instant style →

YOUR SEASON-BY-SEASON GUIDE FOR WORK AND WEEKEND

Produced by Melcher Media

for In Style Books and Time Inc. Home Entertainment

From the editors of *In Style*

Written by Kathleen Fifield

Designed by Studio Usher

instant style

YOUR SEASON-BY-SEASON GUIDE FOR WORK AND WEEKEND

IN STYLE

Managing Editor Charla Lawhon
Executive Editors Martha McCully, Leonora Wiener
Assistant Managing Editor Patrick Moffitt
Deputy Editors Donna Bulseco, Alison Gwinn
Creative Director John Korpics
Photography Director Bradley Young
Fashion Directors Hal Rubenstein, Cynthia Weber Cleary
Accessories Director Alice H. Kim
Market Director Toby Tucker Peters
Senior Style Editor Sydne Bolden
Senior Market Editor Erin Sumwalt
Accessories Editor Brooke Jaffe

President Stephanie George
Publisher Lynette Harrison Brubaker
General Manager Maria Tucci Beckett
Vice President, Brand Development Amy Ford Keohane
Vice President, Public Relations Kristen Jones Connell
Associate Director, Public Relations Katherine Retamozo

IN STYLE BOOKS

Editor, In Style Books Leonora Wiener
Vice President, Brand Development Amy Ford Keohane

Editor, *Instant Style* Alison Gwinn
Fashion Director Cynthia Weber Cleary
Style Editors Sydne Bolden, Ginger Brang Whitenack
Prop Stylist Miako Katoh
Editorial Assistant Rebecca Grice
Imaging Manager Steve Cadicamo
Imaging Specialist Rey Delgado
Production Associate Bijal Saraiya

TIME INC. HOME ENTERTAINMENT

Publisher Richard Fraiman
Executive Director, Marketing Services Carol Pittard
Director, Retail & Special Sales Tom Mifsud
Marketing Director, Branded Businesses Swati Rao
Director, New Product Development Peter Harper
Financial Director Steven Sandonato
Assistant General Counsel Dasha Smith Dwin
Prepress Manager Emily Rabin
Book Production Manager Suzanne Janso
Marketing Manager Victoria Alfonso
Associate Prepress Manager Anne-Michelle Gallero

MELCHER MEDIA

This book was produced by Melcher Media, Inc.
124 West 13th St. / New York, NY 10011 / www.melcher.com

Publisher Charles Melcher
Associate Publisher Bonnie Eldon
Editor in Chief Duncan Bock

Senior Editor Lia Ronnen
Assistant Editor Lauren Nathan
Design Studio Usher
Art Director Naomi Usher
Designer David Seifert
Production Director Andrea Hirsh
Cover photographs David Lawrence
Workbook front cover photograph Time Inc. Digital Studio
Workbook back cover photograph Alex Cao
Special edition covers photograph Saitoshi Saikusa

PUBLISHED BY IN STYLE BOOKS

contents

Introduction

At *In Style*, we pride ourselves on giving readers the first peek of each season's new must-haves, but we also like to share the how-to along with the wow. This book lets us take that practical side a bit further. Whether you're in the market for all-new everything or just fine-tuning a well-established look, you'll find clear, step-by-step advice, outfit by outfit, season by season. Why else should you pick up *Instant Style*? Read on for our top 10 reasons.

—Charla Lawhon, Managing Editor, *In Style*

TWELVE MONTHS OF *IN STYLE* IS SIMPLY NOT ENOUGH Seeing all those celebrities is addictive. We know. That's why you'll find lots of your favorite faces—like Kate Hudson, Salma Hayek, Halle Berry and Gwyneth Paltrow—modeling the looks we love.

YOU FIND SHOPPING ABOUT AS MUCH FUN AS A ROOT CANAL If spending less time at the mall sounds nice, you'll love our guides to what to buy for work, weekend—even destination weddings or business trips.

YOU FIND SHOPPING A LITTLE *TOO* MUCH FUN Impulse buys draining your retirement fund? We'll tell you if you're spending too much. Does your wardrobe have too much personality, too few ready-to-go outfits? Scan our list of style pitfalls.

YOUR LOOK COULD USE A LITTLE DEFINITION Modern-day Audrey? Bohemian luxe? Sporty with a twist? Check out our celebrity style-makers for inspiration.

5 YOU KNOW YOU HAVE A CIRCLE SKIRT AND A CASHMERE T SOMEWHERE, IF ONLY YOU COULD FIND THEM Our four-step closet overhaul will make you a sort-and-purge enthusiast in no time at all.

6 SOMEWHERE BETWEEN CASUAL FRIDAY AND SUITING SEPARATES, THINGS GOT A LITTLE CONFUSING Sometimes today's mix-and-match, high-and-low climate seems too hard. This book will help, with dozens of outfits that show how to put all the pieces together.

7 YOU'RE FEELING A LITTLE BIT GENEROUS IN THE HIPS DEPARTMENT Your starting point with clothes should always be how they flatter your figure. We've got tips to help you downplay—or maximize—your assets.

8 YOU NEED A REASON TO SPLURGE Our list of totally trendproof, worth-the-extra-expense treasures should do the trick.

9 YOU WONDER: WHAT BRA DO I WEAR WITH THAT? Brevity may be the soul of lingerie, but we've got the full scoop on all the underpinnings you need.

10 YOU'VE STOOD IN FRONT OF YOUR CLOSET ON TOO MANY MORNINGS AND FELT THE PANIC RISING Don't sweat it. With this book's advice you'll be on your way to a wardrobe you love in no time. So kick off your heels, put up your feet, and enjoy.

CHAPTER 1

Be Your Own Stylist

GETTING PERSONAL When it comes to style, it's all about you. How you work it. How you own it. Where you borrowed it. And, in a more practical sense, how you narrow down an avalanche of options to those that work for your figure, your coloring, your personality—your life. Of course sometimes (cue hideous dressing room lighting) we all struggle with the very basic question of what looks right on us. To help you clear up any of your own fashion frustrations, we've put together a refresher course on everything from choosing your colors to dressing your age (with a little celebrity inspiration included).

Know Your Own Shape

It's not that some women look good in clothes and others don't. It's about choosing cuts and styles that are right for you

one

IDENTIFY YOUR BODY TYPE You know that voice in your head? The one saying you can't wear those jeans because your hips will look gargantuan in them? Here's where you listen to it, just a little bit, and get a handle on where you fall in the basic range of shapes. Curvy like Salma Hayek? Petite like Eva Longoria? Get ready to compare.

two

ACCENTUATE THE POSITIVE Time to let the angst go. If you didn't have your shape, you'd have another. And they all require some specialized attention to what to wear and how. Check out our celebrity case studies to learn the basics of silhouette and proportion: things like when you need a flare at the hem, a V-neck instead of a crew, or the distraction of ruching or beads up top.

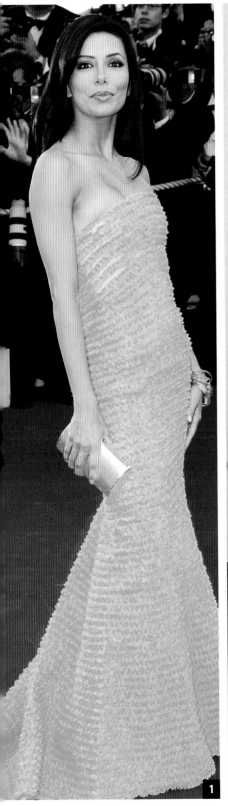

EVA LONGORIA
slender/petite

When you're small-boned and under 5'4", the guiding principles are to wear shapes that don't overwhelm your delicate frame and to avoid too many competing elements in a single outfit.

1> An unbroken vertical line like that created by Eva's long column gown adds the illusion of stature; so does a close, body-hugging fit. And notice how the artful curves of the dress's mermaid shape help draw the eye upward.

2> If you're going for a bold dress like this patterned Cavalli, keep accessories to a minimum. Few can wear ruffles on the rear; here they're offset by the vertical lace-up back. Open heels lengthen legs, but avoid those that look out of proportion with shorter legs.

SALMA HAYEK
curvy/petite

No one could regret a body like this. But because curves can look exaggerated on smaller frames, the skill is in how you play with proportion.

1> Petites like Salma generally look good in high or even Empire waists. Here, her dress also balances her bust with a flare at the hem. Black highlights the play of shapes and is slimming.

2> Fitted, floor-skimming (and thus leg-lengthening) jeans contrasted with a flowing V-neck blouse show her shape with subtle finesse. What wouldn't work as well for her body type: cropped or overly detailed jeans with a tight, crewneck T.

small-busted

So you're not buxom. Who cares? take a natural approach and just add distractions where needed.

1> The technique for smaller-chested women is to create a little drama where others might have heft. The beading on Kate's unstructured cami does the trick under a suit; so would ruching, ruffles or unbuttoning a white shirt a few notches.

2> Not everyone can wear shine as well as trim and tiny Kate. But this metallic gown works well for her shape. In her favor is its Empire waist and the shiny piece of fabric that sits horizontally across her chest, giving the illusion of volume.

DREW BARRYMORE

busty

You don't want to show too much, of course, but like Drew you do need to avoid bulky, overly volu-minous clothes.

1> Never sacrifice your waist. In a shapeless, buttoned-up suit a big bust can make a woman look hefty from shoulder to waist. Drew's better way: stylishly belt-ing her wool suit to create a beau-tiful head-to-toe hourglass.

2> Her solid dress creates a flat-tering vertical line, broken only by the subtly sexy tilt at the top. Nude shoes finish off the sophisticated approach and lengthen legs.

1

2

1

2

BEYONCÉ

curvy

Hiding this kind of shape is never really an option. So be like Beyoncé and play it up.

1> In a metallic gown Beyoncé takes the "if you've got 'em, flaunt 'em" approach. If your curves aren't quite as seamless under a shape-hugging gown, a waist-to-knee body shaper will work wonders.

2> What's accentuating the positive? Form-hugging, cropped pants paired with a midriff-baring blouse. If you wanted the same effect with less, um, impact, lower the pants hem and drop the blouse to the waistline.

QUEEN LATIFAH
full-figured

Fit, color and careful attention to silhouette make outfits come together for someone who's larger.

1> The Queen's rules: Always show a little skin at the neck or décolletage (V-necks are one great option) and make sure you balance looser pieces with others custom-fit for you (note the great line of her pants). In fact, it's worth it to find a tailor you love and factor his or her services into your wardrobe budget.

2> Big prints? Generally not. But color should be in your repertoire. It works in monochrome and with simpler shapes. An Empire waist and long inverted pleat are also clear-cut flatterers.

1

2

CAMERON DIAZ
boyish

We'd surf in a bikini too, if we had Cameron's coltish build. But a little short on curves? Just add ruffle and flow.

1> This white dress would backfire on someone short and stocky, but it's gorgeous on such a slender frame. Ties and bows create the illusion of more of a waist, while ruching enhances the bust. The flared tulle bottom creates an overall eye-catching curve.

2> Corset be damned. Instead of cinching curves into existence, Cameron distracts from her straighter midsection with a wide scoop neck; flowing, asymmetrical hem; ruffles on her shoulder straps; and bows on her shoes.

Know Your Best Colors

People devote entire books to color theory. Here's a three-step plan to finding the shades that bring out the most beautiful you

one — **UNDERSTAND WARM VS. COOL** It's intuitive: Warm colors are the stuff of fire and sunlight—red, yellow and orange. Cool colors are blue, green or violet. Given common hair, eye and skin color combos, most people look best in shades from one side of the spectrum or the other.

two — **TAKE YOUR COLOR TEMPERATURE** Metallics are a fast way to type yourself. Warm types look best in gold jewelry; cool types shimmer in silver. To test, buy foil wrapping paper in gold and in silver and hold a piece of each below your face. Which one brings out the glow?

three — **GET TONAL** Yes, blue is always cooler than orange. But you can find cooler or warmer tones within a color group that work for you. For example, red is cooler if it's closer to violet, warmer if closer to orange. A warm pink is a peachy pink, a cool pink is more mauve.

SELMA BLAIR

NAOMI WATTS

RACHEL MCADAMS

TERI HATCHER

SARAH JESSICA PARKER

VIRGINIA MADSEN

⊕ If you respond to cool...

Chances are your skin has more blue undertones and burns easily.
Your makeup bag boasts a pearly eye shadow or two. **WHAT TO WEAR**
Along with blues and greens, opt for black, gray and deep gem tones.
The best reds on you will be blue-reds like eggplant or burgundy.

HILARY SWANK

JESSICA SIMPSON

EMMY ROSSUM

MARIA BELLO

ROSARIO DAWSON

MICHELLE WILLIAMS

⊕ If warm colors give you that glow...

It's likely that your hair and eyes could be described as "earthy" and that the foundation you buy is more yellow- than pink-based. **WHAT TO WEAR** Those rich spice colors all work for you, as does gold jewelry. Pastels will tend to make your skin look sallow or clash with your hair.

CLAIRE DANES

KATE BECKINSALE

FAITH HILL

KRISTIN DAVIS

JENNIFER CONNELLY

MANDY MOORE

⬆ If you're not getting a reading...

You're neutral, or something like it, since your skin tone falls somewhere between the extremes of blue and yellow undertones. **WHAT TO WEAR** You have a lot of flexibility with color, but when in doubt it sometimes helps to judge a hue by how it brings out your eyes, not your skin.

Know What Suits Your Age

Has your short skirt reached its expiration date? Dressing for your decade is not what it used to be. How to determine what works when

one

LEARN THE RULES A woman in her 20s never wants to look matronly; beware nude pantyhose or pants with pleats. A mom in her 40s should fear looking like she raided her teen's closet. She should cover the midriff and nix the whiskers on the jeans. Minis are off the table after a certain age, and if you're 50 or beyond, watch the sleeveless tops and plunging necklines.

two

FEEL FREE TO BREAK THEM The truth is, strict dictums about what to wear when are fading faster than a botoxed wrinkle. Mostly it comes down to personal transformation. As you age your body changes, yes, but so do your taste, your budget and your lifestyle. Dressing your age is really about making sure your clothes reflect who you are now and upping the quality of your threads year by year.

KATE BOSWORTH, 23

JESSICA ALBA, 25

JESSICA BIEL, 24

EVE, 28

20s

Rules, schmules. You've got permission to experiment.

▶ **BE PLAYFUL** Anything goes when you're a 20-something, from pretty, girlie dresses to edgier ensembles. Take chances, and try unexpected pairings and silhouettes. You might luck into a great look or a new shape for you.

▶ **SHOW SOME LEG** Do it now, before you get older and are looking back and wishing you'd appreciated that body then. The time will pass when you can wear challenging or trendy lengths.

▶ **ADORN YOURSELF** Layer on the bangles, the long necklaces, the bijoux from various bygone eras.

30s

You can wear anything—with sophistication.

▶ **UP THE QUALITY** As your tastes inch upward, start investing in things like a smart black coat or a beautiful day-to-night blazer.

▶ **GET SERIOUS ABOUT FIT** You should have a tailor you trust for things like high-end suits. Jettison trends that don't fit your body type.

▶ **MIX IT UP** Since you can still wear just about anything, don't forget to bring a few wild cards into the dressing room with you now and then.

▶ **EMBRACE SEXY** Suddenly, you have the confidence and authority to undo that next button or pull off a pencil skirt.

GWYNETH PALTROW, 34

CATE BLANCHETT, 37

LUCY LIU, 38

EVA MENDES, 32

HEATHER LOCKLEAR, 45

SHARON STONE, 48

CINDY CRAWFORD, 40

DEMI MOORE, 43

40s

Confidence becomes you—all you need is a little editing.

▶ **INVEST** Buy a few standout items like a designer suit or an embroidered evening coat that you'll wear for years to come.

▶ **GO NO-FRILLS** Steer clear of fussy (ruffles, bows), girlie (little prints, eyelet tops) and matronly (pastel separates, shapeless suits).

▶ **KEEP YOUR EDGE** Combining a few currently cool pieces—embellished heels, a croc bag, a leather blazer—with more classic styles looks great.

▶ **TONE IT** If you're in good shape you can wear almost anything, slinky gown included. Let your body be your guide.

50s

Dress to express yourself. Camouflage as needed.

▶ **ADD YOUR OWN ACCENTS** Splurge on statement pieces. A chunky necklace or signature cuff has more impact than a sedate string of pearls or tennis bracelet.

▶ **DRESS FOR IMPACT** Mono-chromatic outfits are a wise and ageless choice; they look both decisive and dramatic.

▶ **KEEP CASUAL CURRENT** Look for coordinated pieces in fabrics that layer (and travel) well. Try a big watch, leather sneaks or a cashmere hoodie.

▶ **PLAY WITH COLOR** Your skin and hair change as you get older, so you'll want to find the shades that work best for you now.

ANJELICA HUSTON, 55

MARY STEENBURGEN, 53

OPRAH WINFREY, 52

SIGOURNEY WEAVER, 56

GOLDIE HAWN, 60

STOCKARD CHANNING, 62

ALI MACGRAW, 67

JANE FONDA, 68

60s

Elegance becomes you. Feel free to splurge—you deserve it.

▶ **LOOK FOR MODERN CUTS**
You're too self-assured for trends, but you'll still want to keep the cut of your suits and trousers trim and of-the-moment.

▶ **GO FOR GUILTY PLEASURES**
A little shine can flatter your skin, and the richness of fur trim or brocade looks right on you now.

▶ **COVER WHEN YOU HAVE TO**
You know if you still feel like showing off your legs. As for arms, keep 'em toned, or, for evening, throw on a chic wrap.

Know Your Personal Style

Fun and flirty? Sporty chic? Quietly sophisticated? Take a look at these stars—then court your own look that says head-to-toe cool

one

GET INSPIRED So maybe Chanel haute couture and vintage Valentino aren't your personal standbys. We're still betting you'll respond to something in our lineup of celebrities who have strong fashion personalities.

two

DEFINE YOUR LOOK Chances are, there's a style definition that clicks with you. On your way to finding your look, think about the things you love to wear—the pieces in your closet that feel right when you put them on—and those it might be time to let go of.

three

SHOP STRATEGICALLY Sure, every wardrobe needs variety, but every piece you're eyeballing on the rack should be run through your style filter. Keeping some consistency will lead to a wardrobe that works together and says something about you.

SCARLETT
JOHANSSON

the bombshell

▶ So young. So Old Hollywood. So comfortable with a satin train and seriously lush lips. Scarlett's siren look speaks to impact and the love of mesmerizing a crowd. Notice how unafraid she is to wear look-at-me jewel tones in a setting that normally features a sea of shimmery neutrals and black. Also note how much she likes being a girl, and how her dress choices—or even her knockaround jeans and Ts—play up her God-given, hourglass assets. P.S. She's often seen in diamonds.

SARAH JESSICA
PARKER

ladylike

▶ Her character on *Sex and the City* launched a thousand trends and she herself once wore a tutu to the Golden Globes—and a pair of jazz shorts and bustier to a major fashion awards ceremony. But recently SJP has become the princess of retro chic (with a twist). Elegant, fifties cocktail dresses are one favorite element of her polished and very "done" look, though she tends to add a creative personal signature—like a single standout jewel or a shot of color in her shoes.

←

SIENNA MILLER
bohemian luxe

▶ The girl just gets it: the trend, the reference, how to spin a look with a vintage extra or slightly unexpected pairing. When it comes to her masterful mix and how she accessorizes, there's more than a little gypsy in her soul. Sienna likes things that go clink when she walks; big, unstructured bags; boots; little jackets; and jeans, jeans, jeans. But with all her layers there's cohesion too: She sticks to classic colors and lets her baubles make the noise.

JOY BRYANT
all-american

▶ The onetime model admittedly loves fashion—as well as those plunging Vs. But there's also something simple, straightforward and exceedingly confident about her ever-changing choices. Even with all her statement dressing she looks comfortable, almost sporty. Check out accents like her aviator glasses, flats and hip-slung leather belt. We'll call it fun without the fuss—all-American in the best sense of the term.

←

JENNIFER ANISTON
the natural

▶ Whether she's wearing vintage Valentino (far left) or a simple tank and skirt, her look is cool without ever being contrived. She's got a sleek, uncluttered way with modern pieces and relies on neutrals and a perfect fit to make her biggest impact. From her jewelry to her fabric picks, there's no excess, no confusion and nothing that takes the focus away from her natural assets: her beautiful hair, skin and body.

JENNIFER LOPEZ

glam

▶ Too much is never enough when you are talking about Jennifer's no-holds-barred look. Feminine flourishes dominate her arsenal. She'll combine a flare, a ruffle, cuffs and a mink faster than another woman would ask, "Is it OK to mix gold and silver?" What keeps her look truly glamorous and not merely eclectic is her unified approach to color and the way her clothes flatter her body. This look doesn't happen by accident. There's method to her vamp, and a ladylike poise too.

RACHEL BILSON

girl next door

▶ Adorable in a feminine, fitted dress, sporty-chic in youthful basics, this young star makes simplicity a recognizable signature. Just the fact that she almost always eschews jewelry makes a subtle statement we like. It also separates her from the show-everything-and-layer-it-on teen flock. Fresh, young, yet proper too, Rachel gives polish a sweet shine.

ANGELINA JOLIE

sultry

▶ Favoring elegant cuts and black and white, she has developed a clean and sophisticated style for evening that telegraphs power and control. (Think of it as the flip-side to her more casual daytime jeans-and-boots look: She doesn't need any frills interfering with the business at hand.) Sexy tuxedos are one red-carpet favorite; wearing them with a classic white shirt and pumps only adds to the authority. To make white look knowing, not innocent, she combines a sleek shape with red satin accents.

HALLE BERRY
the goddess

▶ We've seen her to-ing and fro-ing from the gym, looking casually hip in sweat suits. But it's when she takes that killer body and puts it in a dress that Halle's true style imprint appears. From the ornate and curve-hugging gowns she favors to the regal poise she achieves in wearing them, her strength is in her feminine power and physical confidence. Hips and shoulders are favorite focal points; so are her arms, which she highlights with supersize sparkling cuffs and bangles.

CHAPTER 2

Edit Your Wardrobe

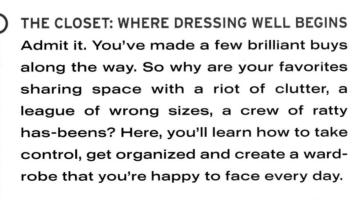

○ **THE CLOSET: WHERE DRESSING WELL BEGINS**
Admit it. You've made a few brilliant buys along the way. So why are your favorites sharing space with a riot of clutter, a league of wrong sizes, a crew of ratty has-beens? Here, you'll learn how to take control, get organized and create a wardrobe that you're happy to face every day.

Step 1: Clean Up

FOLLOW OUR PAINLESS PLAN TO CREATE ORDER AND HARMONY IN THE RACKS

Prep

Your closet, like your clothes, should be seasonal. Move your off-season threads out or to the back of the closet, but make sure you store them correctly. Clean everything—insects such as moths are attracted to dirt and odors. And protect your duds from dust and light by storing them in hanging canvas bags.

Plan

You know that compulsively honest friend (or mother or sister)? Call her up and offer to be her assistant organizer next Friday if she'll be yours this Saturday. That second opinion could be critical as you tackle the task of deciding what items in your wardrobe still look good on you. What you should have on hand for your upcoming date: a full-length mirror, a box of heavy-duty garbage bags, labels and lots of hangers. The most serious closet overhauls can also benefit from a rolling rack.

Sort

You'll be making four piles: keepers, items that need attention (from the dry cleaner or a tailor), clothes to be tossed, and pieces you'll donate to charity or resell. So get your garbage bags and labels ready, and be prepared to try on every single item of clothing to determine if it still fits and if you still love it.

NECESSARY REPAIRS

Attack your "needs attention" pile and get your shoes, bags and clothes ready for their close-up.

1> Hit the tailor with the pants that need to be hemmed or the jackets that need a nip to the waist. Visit the dry cleaner with anything less than clean and crisp. Take almost perfect cashmere sweaters to a reweaver. (It's not worth the cost for lesser fibers.)

2> Resole your standby loafers or replace the heels on your party-circuit sandals (a good shoe-repair shop can also add, remove, shorten or lengthen straps).

3> Create a repair and maintenance kit to have on hand for on-the-spot fixes. Fill with a lint brush, safety pins, a soft sponge to remove deodorant, sewing needles, sharp scissors, light and dark spools of thread and extra buttons. Also add shoe polish, plus a brush or sponge shiner.

Step 2: Organize

USE THESE STORAGE TRICKS TO HELP YOU FIND ITEMS—FAST

scarves
Baskets make great holding places for knit scarves, hats and gloves. Place fragile items like silk scarves or leather gloves in a shallow drawer, or in their own storage box with a label and lid.

belts
Hang these on a row of hooks at eye level to make them easy to reach (and quick to replace). Another plus: Buckles won't scratch as they might in a drawer.

jewelry
Boxes are fine for earrings and a couple of bracelets, but keep them sparsely filled to avoid tangles. Or pin necklaces and earrings to a bulletin board.

shoes
First, don't scatter them on the floor. They'll get dusty and lose their mates. Built-in shelves or hanging canvas shelves are ideal. But if you lack space, store shoes in stackable clear boxes or in their original boxes with a digital or Polaroid photo of them taped to the front.

bags
They should rest upright, so line them up on a shelf or in cubbyholes by size and occasion. Stuff with tissue paper.

Step 3: Style

AS THE FOG CLEARS, SCAN YOUR KEEPERS FOR THESE WARDROBE SHORTCOMINGS

Pitfalls

1> Do you have too many basics and not enough thrills or frills?

2> Too many solids, too few prints? Too much black, not enough color?

3> Could a ruffle here or a flare there balance all the tailored pants?

4> Would something beaded, metallic or lacy bring some texture to the mix?

5> Are your outfits a little too predictable? Is there a range of silhouettes?

CREATE OUTFITS; GET INSPIRED Walk into any designer's studio and, along with the rolling racks and track lighting, you'll find a couple of familiar sights: their look books and inspiration boards, visual ways to present their collections and gather images that inspire them. After restyling your own clothes, create a look book of your new outfits by shooting digital or Polaroid photos of them for reference and mounting them in a binder. An inspiration board (like the one at left) is a collage of looks you love (and might want to imitate). Tack up pages from your favorite fashion magazines as well as things like postcards, snapshots or color swatches that remind you of a shade or mood that speaks to your style.

Step 4: Voila!

YOU'RE CLOSE. JUST FOLLOW THESE FIVE FINAL TIPS FOR THE GET-HAPPY CLOSET

1 UPGRADE YOUR HANGERS

Take sagging wire hangers that aren't easy to rifle through to your dry cleaner. Try plastic or wood instead.

2 GROUP LIKE WITH LIKE

Once you've got skirts with skirts, blouses with blouses, and pants with pants, subdivide by color, then style and fabric. To prevent wrinkles, leave at least one-inch of rod space between items.

3 GET CREATIVE WITH SPACE

Would a built-in bureau or shelves help you maximize space in a tight corner? Could you fit double hanging rods above and below for shirts and pants?

4 TAME YOUR SHELVES

Buy bins or baskets to hold swimsuits and exercise gear; clip on plastic dividers to help keep your stacks of sweaters or Ts in place.

5 ADD BOUTIQUE TOUCHES

Paint the back wall a bold hue, install vintage hooks, or hang a pendant light. (Adding a little scent—cedar, jasmine or lavender—will keep things fresh.)

CHAPTER 3

Fall/Winter Wardrobe

TEAMWORK We just love it when a plan comes together: when a tweed blazer looks just right with menswear trousers or a chocolate pencil skirt; when the splurge-worthy pumps elevate your little black dress and your boot-cut pants. With such style harmony in mind, this chapter outlines the essential fall and winter pieces, item by item, shape by shape. Take a look at the new basics, then find ideas for combining them in fresh, fabulous outfits that can take you from corporate seminar to evening soirée.

Daytime Capsule Wardrobe

Wool coat? Check. Tall boots? Check. We're not saying one style fits all, but these are the basic pieces that *we* couldn't live without

FIRST THINGS FIRST It's like learning addition before algebra: You can't skimp on the fundamentals if you're trying to build a closet of perfect clothes. That's why we're starting off with a back-to-basics reality check: a list of the necessary mix-and-match pieces for day that are the essential underpinnings of great style. Do you have those black wool pants—tailored just so—that take you from your Thursday A.M. meeting to your Thursday evening book group, with compliments along the way? What kind of shape is your instant-impact white shirt in by now? What about your sophisticated leather work tote? Take a moment to check off what you already have and what you may still need. You'll want to buy the basics in the best quality you can afford and go from there.

☑ knee-length wool coat

☑ white shirt

☑ jacket to match skirt and pants

☑ v-neck sweater

☑ work dress

☑ leather tote

☑ black bootcut pants

☑ everyday purse

☑ a-line skirt

☑ flats

☑ jeans

☑ to-the-knee boots

☑ cardigan

☑ black pumps

Coats

CHOOSE THE SHAPE THAT MAKES YOUR BEST ENTRANCE

BELTED

WHAT WE LOVE
Classic, sophisticated and ideal for a range of body types. The belt accentuates (or creates) a waist.
WEAR IT WELL
It goes with almost anything, but make sure skirt hems do not peek out the bottom.

ROBE

WHAT WE LOVE
It's relaxed but classy; the shape is so elegant that it can stand as an evening coat.
WEAR IT WELL
Make sure the fabric is supple, so it drapes rather than clumps.

KNEE-LENGTH

WHAT WE LOVE
Tailored takes never look dated and work for women of all heights.
WEAR IT WELL
Color can be the ideal complement to a wardrobe full of browns and blacks.

DOUBLE-BREASTED

WHAT WE LOVE
Its linear cool makes it great with menswear trousers or a white skirt.
WEAR IT WELL
Double-breasted styles are warmest but not great for curvy/busty types.

looks we love

PRINCESS

WHAT WE LOVE
That retro vibe.
Works ideally for pear
shapes or (with its wide
collar) bigger busts.
WEAR IT WELL
The coat's so romantic,
it's best to wear it
with modern shapes.

MILITARY

WHAT WE LOVE
These structured styles
have rakish charm
and instant impact.
WEAR IT WELL
Fewer gold buttons
and martial details will
add style longevity.

RENEE ZELLWEGER IN A CLASSIC KNEE-LENGTH

Weather Beaters

WHAT TO LOOK FOR WHEN YOU NEED A REALLY WARM TOPPER

CASHMERE The wondrous insulating properties of Mongolian goat hair mean greater warmth at a lighter weight. But cashmere is more delicate than wool; a coat in a blend of both will wear better and is a good choice for cold, damp climates.

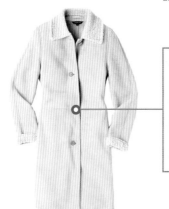

SHEARLING Soft and supple, this lamb pelt (technically considered a fur) is unbeatable in the cold. In a coat, it also tends to be more comfortable than sheepskin, which weighs more but isn't necessarily warmer. Both are rain-resistant, though not waterproof.

FUR When it comes to keeping you toasty, not all furs are created equal. Sable is the warmest—and most expensive. Other pricey but effective insulators are mink, chinchilla, fox and nutria. Rabbit and beaver cost less but are not as warm.

LEATHER Those biker dudes know at least one thing: Skin is best for blocking the wind. Many leathers are water-resistant, but some may stain in the rain. You'll need a lining to wear beyond autumn and, most likely, a warmer coat for deep winter.

SYNTHETIC Man-made insulators such as Primaloft, Thermolite or Gore-Tex are less bulky than down but will still keep you warm at minus 10 degrees. Plus, they dry faster and can be sewn into more form-fitting shapes than their natural competitor.

DOWN The warmest puffer will be the one filled most densely with this fluffy fowl stuff. To judge, look for a "fill power" of 600 or higher (and consider if you're tall enough to wear that much volume). Also, make sure the outer layer or shell is waterproof since down itself dries slowly.

Suits

THREE WISE BUYS THAT TAKE CARE OF ALL KINDS OF BUSINESS

WORK

WHAT WE LOVE
Subtlety and a perfect
fit are powerful things;
just add polished extras.

WEAR IT WELL
Look for high-quality,
lightweight wool that
doesn't cling or have
any shine.

DRESSY

WHAT WE LOVE
Endless options.
Jacket on, jacket off,
bow-front cami or
no cami at all.

WEAR IT WELL
Velvet or velveteen
will hide figure flaws
better than thinner,
shinier nighttime
fabrics like satin.

looks we love

LADYLIKE

WHAT WE LOVE
Sit back and let the shape and details make your outfit for you.
WEAR IT WELL
Look for extras like covered buttons, peplum waist or pleats that fall flat as a doily.

KATE WINSLET IN COOL WHITE, SANS SHIRT

One Suit, Four Ways

TWO PIECES OF LIGHTWEIGHT WOOL PROVE SERIOUSLY VERSATILE

1 →

CORPORATE CHIC
Ruffles and a print add
the right zest to more
conservative navy
stripes.

2 →

AFTER HOURS
Silk and metallics
dress up a suit
for evening.

3 →

CLASS ACT
The key to mixing
up pieces of a suit is
pairing them with fabric
or color opposites.

4 →

SUNDAY BRUNCH
If your suit jacket
is shapely enough,
it'll look right even
with jeans.

Skirts

THE MUST-HAVES MIX FLARE WITH TAPER AND SWEET WITH SEXY

PENCIL

WHAT WE LOVE
Tapering past hips, it
can create curves where
there aren't any.
WEAR IT WELL
Equally sexy or shapely
shoes, such as pumps,
are required footwear.

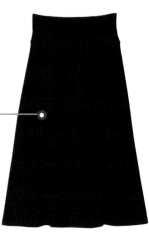

A-LINE

WHAT WE LOVE
Like boot-cut pants, its
slight flare flatters any-
one with a little hip.
WEAR IT WELL
It should hit at the
midpoint of the knee;
longer looks dowdy.

PLEATED

WHAT WE LOVE
Top-to-bottom pleats
add movement to this
always classic style.
WEAR IT WELL
You need fabric with an
easy drape; try wool crêpe,
silk blends or rayon.

FLARE

WHAT WE LOVE
Let's say you have a great
waist but "athletic"
thighs; this one's for you.
WEAR IT WELL
Avoid any length that
hits at the midpoint of the
calf; try slightly below.

FULL

WHAT WE LOVE
A great cocktail party
staple, it's good cover
for wider hips or thighs.
WEAR IT WELL
Balance is everything:
Pair its playful volume
with a more fitted top.

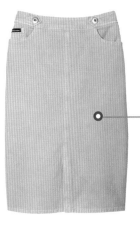

TROUSER

WHAT WE LOVE
It's straight and sleek
without being as wildly
curvaceous as the pencil.
WEAR IT WELL
Leave a little skin or
stocking between the
hem and the top of a boot.

SELMA BLAIR IN A PLEATED PENCIL SKIRT

Shirts and Blouses

WHAT TO BUTTON UP, FROM MENSWEAR CUFFS TO ROMANTIC RUFFLES

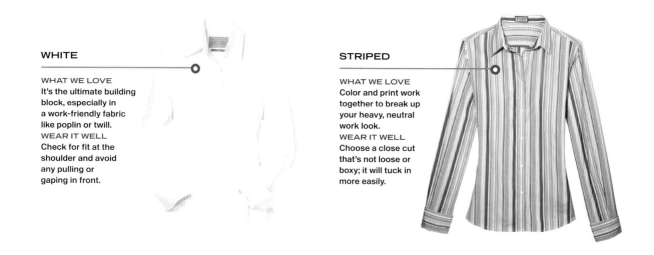

WHITE

WHAT WE LOVE
It's the ultimate building block, especially in a work-friendly fabric like poplin or twill.
WEAR IT WELL
Check for fit at the shoulder and avoid any pulling or gaping in front.

STRIPED

WHAT WE LOVE
Color and print work together to break up your heavy, neutral work look.
WEAR IT WELL
Choose a close cut that's not loose or boxy; it will tuck in more easily.

LONG-SLEEVE T

WHAT WE LOVE
Add a few strong accessories and a jacket on top, and you're work-ready.
WEAR IT WELL
Choose a tailored fit over a boxy one, which rests close to your hip, with no gap under the arm.

RUFFLE FRONT

WHAT WE LOVE
An open neckline makes ruffles an option for even the well-endowed.
WEAR IT WELL
That's a lot of shirt; go for a sleeker bottom (tuxedo pants, pencil skirt).

looks we love

ROMANTIC

WHAT WE LOVE
A blouse with prim details looks great in a gauzy fabric, which adds flow and sex appeal.

WEAR IT WELL
Contrast is called for; try it with edgy cigarette pants and spiky heels.

SHEER

WHAT WE LOVE
If you like camisoles but they don't like your arms, a sheer top is ideal.

WEAR IT WELL
The underlayer should look intentional; a nude cotton cami won't cut it.

KATIE HOLMES IN A CRISP WHITE SHIRT

One Blouse, Four Ways

LAYER IT! A CHIFFON PRINT GOES LADYLIKE—OR HIP AND BOHEMIAN

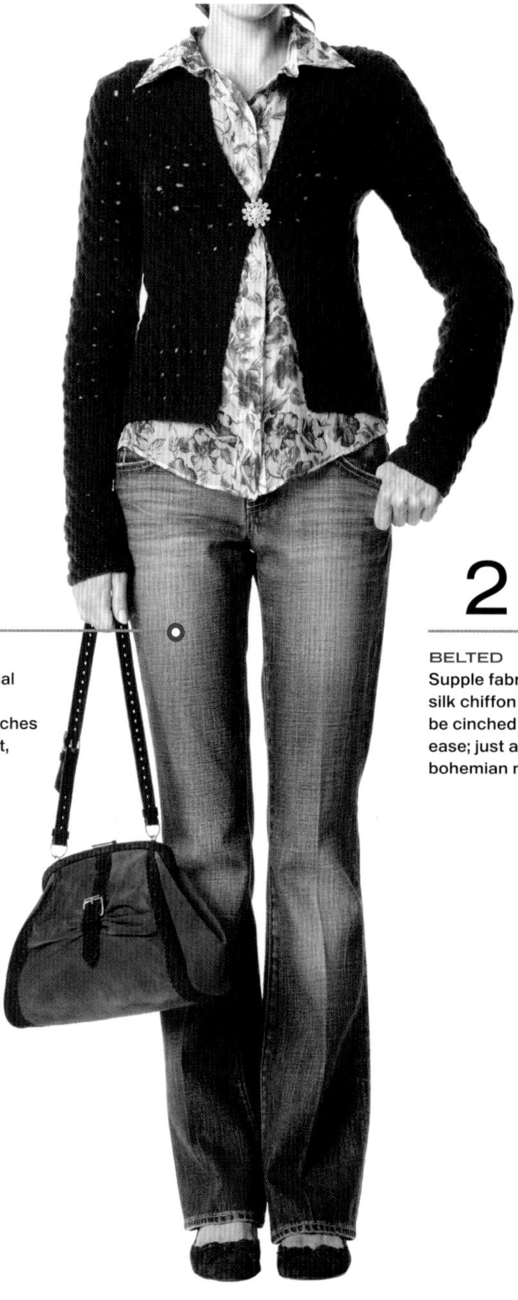

1 →

WEEKENDER
Make it très casual
with a crocheted
sweater that matches
the feminine print,
plus faded jeans.

2 →

BELTED
Supple fabrics like
silk chiffon can
be cinched with
ease; just add
bohemian mien.

3 →

DRESS-UP
A pencil skirt plus a pretty blouse always works, but adding a sweater and layering necklaces makes it signature.

4 →

WORK CASUAL
Experiment with wearing your blouse under a variety of sweater lengths and shapes.

Pants

THE CUT, THE FABRIC, THE STYLES TO LIVE IN NOW

BOOT-CUT

WHAT WE LOVE
The slight flare, starting
at the knee, offsets
fullness at the hips.
WEAR IT WELL
To lengthen legs, leave
as long as possible
(tailor to your heels).

TWEED

WHAT WE LOVE
They're pretty with
earth and gem tones;
thick fabric with a
lining hides bulges.
WEAR IT WELL
Skip the pleats; flat
fronts are the most
current and flattering.

CIGARETTE

WHAT WE LOVE
They offer guaranteed
edge, and these pants
cry out for heels.
WEAR IT WELL
Always wear a fuller top
with a skinny pant to
create balance.

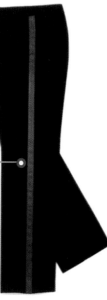

TUXEDO

WHAT WE LOVE
That stripe up the side
signals these aren't
your ho-hum go-to's.
WEAR IT WELL
A touch of Lycra—between
2 and 6 percent—adds just
enough stretch to wool.

looks we love

CORDUROY

WHAT WE LOVE
Comfortable and durable, they work in offices where jeans are verboten.

WEAR IT WELL
Beware any kind of tapered leg. Cords look best in a boot-cut.

CROPPED

WHAT WE LOVE
These new staples have a gamine appeal and lots of impact.

WEAR IT WELL
If pairing with tall boots, the hem should cover the top of the boot.

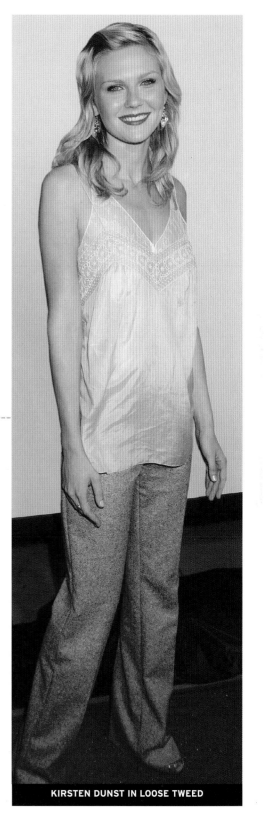

KIRSTEN DUNST IN LOOSE TWEED

Beyond Basic

BREAKING DOWN THE LOOK AND FIT OF THE PERFECT BLACK WOOL PANT

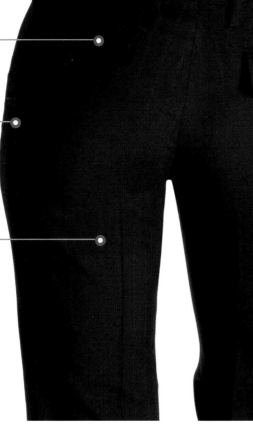

BELT LOOPS

They don't necessitate
an actual belt, unless
you feel like one.

BACK POCKETS

The lining here, or in
any pocket, should never
show through. If it does,
have a tailor remove it.

HIPS

They should be your first
consideration. Pants
should just skim, not cling,
where you're widest. If
you're between sizes, buy
the pair that fits your hips,
then tailor the waist.

FIT

Wool trousers should show
your shape without bagging
but also shouldn't be tight
across the derrière—no
pulling or tugging allowed.

WAIST

For most, a slightly lower-riding waistband (an inch below the belly button) is the most flattering.

FRONT

For style points as well as the best fit, look for a flat, not pleated, front.

RISE

Otherwise known as crotch length. If it's teen-star tiny, the pants will be uncomfortable. But don't go too long either; you'll look dowdy and cut off valuable leg length.

SIDE POCKETS

These should lie flat, to avoid drawing attention to the hips. If they gap the pants may be too small, or pockets may need to be sewn shut.

LEG

A nice drape means no clinging or pulling; they should have a straight line from hip to hem.

HEM

Choose a length based on the heel height you wear most often to work. In front, let the hem rest right on the top of the foot. Avoid very deep breaks. In the back, aim to cover most of your heel.

Sweaters

CLASSY MEETS COZY: THE SIX WEAVES OR SHAPES YOU NEED

TURTLENECK

WHAT WE LOVE
It's cool but serious,
like Audrey Hepburn, and
goes with everything.

WEAR IT WELL
Style with long, dangling
earrings that add flow
to the high, static neck.

V-NECK

WHAT WE LOVE
Its universally flatter-
ing neckline makes
room for a blouse
underneath.

WEAR IT WELL
A wide V distracts
from narrow shoul-
ders and balances
pear-shaped figures.

CARDIGAN

WHAT WE LOVE
Comfy and endlessly
versatile, it looks
great in a fitted, not
boxy, cut.

WEAR IT WELL
A slightly shorter
version will sit nicely
atop waistbands.

LONG BELTED

WHAT WE LOVE
The length adds a
new silhouette to
your wardrobe, plus
cover-up power.

WEAR IT WELL
Swap a rugged leather
(or sleek patent) belt to
make the look your own.

looks we love

OVERSIZE

WHAT WE LOVE
A cowl neck and bell
sleeves mix up a closet
of classic shapes.

WEAR IT WELL
Avoid too-long arms,
since you can't push
up this type of sleeve.

SHRUG

WHAT WE LOVE
It highlights shoulders
and waist and adds
flair to cotton camis.

WEAR IT WELL
Works best over a
fitted top or a waist-
emphasizing dress.

HILARY SWANK IN A SEXY TWIN SET

One Sweater, Four Ways

A LONG CARDIGAN PROVES IT CAN BE MORE THAN JUST COZY

1 →

OFFICE SET
A structured cardigan
makes a creative and
comfortable stand-in
for your work jackets.

2 →

JUST DRINKS
The sweater's
length provides
a nice balance to
all the leg you're
showing in those
fall shorts.

3 →

MOVIE NIGHT
Part security blanket,
part presence. The long
sweater feels stylish
and easy with jeans.

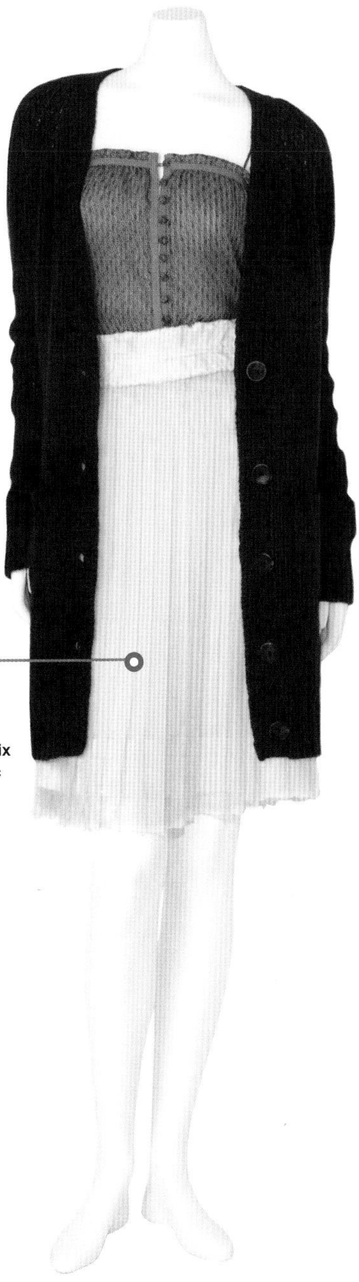

4 →

**DINNER
RESERVATIONS**
Black and white is
always chic; this mix
of shape and fabric
turns playful too.

Jackets

THEY COMPLETE YOU. LEARN WHICH TO HAVE ON HAND

BASIC BLAZER

WHAT WE LOVE
It's the ultimate in wearability, especially in a seasonless lightweight wool.

WEAR IT WELL
Look for one with shape and a three- to four-button front.

FEMININE

WHAT WE LOVE
It uses serious girl power to instantly build outfits around basic black.

WEAR IT WELL
A fitted waist helps a jacket work with long or flared skirts.

TWEED

WHAT WE LOVE
Like houndstooth or bouclé, its texture makes it pair well with solids.

WEAR IT WELL
Fabric opposites also look fresh; try a top or skirt in silk or chiffon.

VELVET

WHAT WE LOVE
A special fabric that you don't have to worry about; that's no-fuss perfection.

WEAR IT WELL
Jeans and heels plus a velvet jacket look festive but unfussy; or throw it over a silk shift.

MILITARY

WHAT WE LOVE
Don the brass with anything from jeans to a pencil skirt.

WEAR IT WELL
Don't overdo the accessories; this one makes a statement on its own.

CROPPED

WHAT WE LOVE
The shrunken look gets a retro update with bracelet sleeves.

WEAR IT WELL
Try with a femme dress or, against type, a ribbed tank and trousers.

JENNIFER ANISTON IN A FITTED BLAZER

One Jacket, Three Ways

A SHAPELY SELF-STARTER BRINGS A TROUSER OR SKIRT TO LIFE

1 →

DAY TO EVENING
With such a shapely jacket on top, you can go with a more loosely cut skirt and blouse. Colored bags add personality.

2 →

WEEKEND WARRIOR
You can't go wrong with jeans and a little jacket, but do it best with a printed top and beads.

looks we love

3 →

BACK TO WORK
With basics like tweed trousers, styling is everything: Wear your collar out for a change, and try a double-wide waist-defining belt.

ELLE MACPHERSON IN A JEANS JACKET

Jeans

SIMPLIFY THE SEARCH FOR THE (NEXT) PERFECT PAIR

TROUSER

WHAT WE LOVE
The cut gives denim a new sophistication and suits most body types.
WEAR IT WELL
Great with nubby little jackets; make sure the pockets lie flat at the side.

HIGH-BACK

WHAT WE LOVE
Coverage. We were tiring of glimpsing everyone's thong.
WEAR IT WELL
Look for a low rise in front. Stretch also helps close the back gap.

BOOT-CUT

WHAT WE LOVE
It's a great cut for all; up a pair's versatility by avoiding funky washes.
WEAR IT WELL
From the rear, widely spaced or small pockets can make your behind look big.

SKINNY

WHAT WE LOVE
Show off your legs in the only style in which a tapered leg is right.
WEAR IT WELL
The no-flare bottom means they work tucked into boots or with heels.

looks we love

CROPPED

WHAT WE LOVE
As flexible as they are fun, crops say modern-day minx.
WEAR IT WELL
Tall boots always work, but so can flats or some heels (without stockings).

RELAXED

WHAT WE LOVE
Your super comfortable, Saturday A.M. standbys can have some give.
WEAR IT WELL
Avoid the drag by shortening these to match your sneaks or flat boots.

MOLLY SIMS LEAVES THEM LONG

One Pair, Four Ways

A CUTE PAIR OF CROPPED JEANS CAN TAKE YOU FROM FUNKY TO SOPHISTICATED

1→

DOWNTOWN BOUND
Like bow-front metallic
flats, cropped jeans can
look cool but kind of
sweet too, with chains
and a jersey top.

2→

COUNTRY ESCAPE
Go antiquing in 'em,
with a long cardigan,
ribbed tank and
slouchy boots that
make the tuck easy.

3 →

HUSTLE AND FLOW
For a night out while
the weather's still
warm, add the unex-
pected baby-doll top
and sky-high heels.

4 →

CLASS ACTION
Crops add cheeky
contrast to the more
proper bow-tie blouse,
fitted jacket and lady-
like peep-toes.

Bags

YOU NEED STYLE PLUS PRACTICALITY IN YOUR DAYTIME COMPANION

HANDHELD

WEAR IT WELL
It demands attention, hanging there on your wrist. Choose a neutral-friendly hue like red or green, or one with buckles or other details.

OBLONG

WEAR IT WELL
Thin and long, it makes a great day-to-night contender. And bags that tuck under the arm flatter wide hips.

HOBO

WEAR IT WELL
Laid-back cool, plus plenty of room for all of your daily essentials. But the bigger the bag, the less appropriate for work.

DRAWSTRING

WEAR IT WELL
The tapered top can rein in a hobo. Just be sure there's some interior organization so you're not rooting when your cell phone rings.

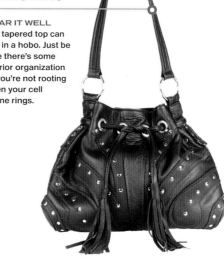

looks we love

ATTACHÉ

WEAR IT WELL
Big hold-everything bags have trumped this classic in recent seasons, but the slim style, plus a handbag, could simplify your work life.

CRESCENT

WEAR IT WELL
Ladylike but modern, the shape provides depth and lots of holding space without getting gigantic. A good pick for smaller women.

REESE WITHERSPOON GOES HANDHELD

Shoes

THESE SHAPES CAN TAKE YOU FAR AND WIDE

LOAFER PUMPS

WEAR THEM WELL
Menswear-inspired day basics, with a kitten or tall stacked heel. Great for straight or A-line skirts; ideal with wide wool or tweed trousers.

POINTED TOE FLATS

WEAR THEM WELL
Skimmers work well with both long and short skirts and slim trousers. If you're petite avoid wearing them with midcalf lengths.

CLASSIC PUMPS

WEAR THEM WELL
Nearly mandatory for a pencil skirt and always right with suits. With pants you'll get the leggiest look by letting just the toe peek out.

KITTEN HEELS

WEAR THEM WELL
This is the must-have work shoe, either with a pointed toe or in a classic d'Orsay cut. Rich fabrics and textures will enliven understated threads.

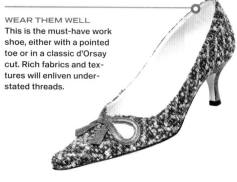

BALLERINA FLATS

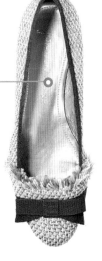

WEAR THEM WELL
Part darling, part
doyenne, they work
with cropped pants
or, if your legs are
thin, full skirts.

ANKLE BOOTS

WEAR THEM WELL
The latest shorties beg
to be noticed with color,
grommets and ties.
Edgy with skinny pants
and downright radical
(read: risky) with skirts.

TALL BOOTS

WEAR THEM WELL
Adding edge to work
basics (and making
knee-length skirts
bearable in winter),
they're comfy too,
if you choose a stacked
heel and round toe.

FLAT BOOTS

WEAR THEM WELL
Equestrian yet rocker,
they work best with
casual pants or skirts.
If your thighs can
handle the attention,
tuck your jeans inside.

Great Work Looks

ADD SOME STANDOUT ACCESSORIES AND CREATE HEAD-TO-TOE STYLE

HIDDEN ASSETS
Get creative with what goes under your suit. Even no-nonsense pinstripes can handle a kicky sweater and checkered mules.

HIS AND HERS
Cropped wool trousers take the stuffiness out of traditional menswear touches, like the striped shirt and tie.

OFFICE ROMANCE
Always balance a fuller skirt with some definition at the waist; belting a longer sweater does just the trick.

ANGLING
A bold geometric print goes down easy when kept below the belt and paired with a fitted cashmere sweater.

3

4

CASUAL FRIDAY
If you're lucky enough to get away with jeans, stay stylish, not sloppy, with a blazer and kitten heels. Instant updater: the silk tie as belt.

CREATIVE TEAM
Pros know to subtly mix textures—a tweed skirt with a beaded cardigan and Victorian-lace blouse—in the same head-to-toe look.

STAND OUT
The best fall looks pair classic and current: wool with unexpected colors like violet and lime, a V-neck and a beaded silk belt.

TOP EARNER
Surprisingly versatile: the fitted white wool blazer. It makes a great foil to darker wools and knits.

7

8

Great Weekend Looks

BUILD ON THE BASICS TO DELIVER READY-TO-GO OPTIONS FOR EVERY NEED

INDIE FILM
A mini can handle layering up top, if the pieces are short enough and go in at the waist. Keep it classy with flats or flat leather boots.

TEXAS HOLD 'EM
Remember belts? Often neglected, they're essential for adding shape to chunky fall pieces. And how cool is that big, bad buckle?

SOCCER AUNT
Buy a pair of slightly retro, low leather lace-ups: your "dressy" sneakers will quickly become weekend favorites.

3

HOUSE HUNTING
Khakis don't need to disappear when it's chilly. Wear them with tailored layers and neo-preppy accents all fall long.

4

DRINKS FIRST
Denim and metallic have been together since disco days. But limit yourself to one piece of metal; gold shoes here would be overkill.

5

GRABBING COFFEE
A hoodie sweater and cool crops instantly alter the mood of a plaid wool jacket. Let a thin knit scarf add playful contrast.

6

AT THE AUCTION
Chaps? No. But a few equestrian details—riding-inspired boots, vest or gloves—add instant class. (Red accents alone add zest to browns.)

SKATE DATE
The sporty look works best when you layer it on. And don't be afraid of white; in a heavy fabric it's virtually seasonless.

Evening Capsule Wardrobe

From the little black dress and pendant necklace to the sweet jacket and glittery shoes, we've got your must-have evening pieces

SENSIBLE MEETS SENSATIONAL When it comes to fashion, we're nocturnal creatures, often saving our very best looks for when the sun goes down. After all, there are expectations to be met: that we'll turn heads over a candlelight dinner, stand out amid a sea of finery at our friend's wedding, or make the right impression at the office holiday party. And while it's tempting to run out and buy a new dress each time another invite arrives, the best approach is a mix-and-match evening wardrobe, not a closet full of one-offs. Such collections tend to evolve over time, but we have a few ideas to get you started: our evening capsule wardrobe, followed by outfits for every occasion.

little black dress

long earrings

silk or satin skirt

pendant necklace

satin camisole

evening clutch

jacket

glittery evening bag

black tuxedo pants

metallic sandals

velvet pants

evening pumps

The Little Black Dress

THE ULTIMATE CHAMELEON SHOWS THE POWER OF ACCESSORIES

1 →

SO GENTEEL
A cropped jacket
with ruffles plus
ladylike pumps and a
dainty clutch make
this ensemble worthy
of a cocktail party
or wedding.

2 →

HAUTE STUFF
With a major statement
piece like a fox
(or faux) shrug, not
much else is needed.
Just add sparkly cuffs
and lace-up heels.

looks we love

3 →

SIMPLY SEXY
The more streamlined
your dress and extras,
the wilder your shoes
can be. If they're
open-toe, always
skip stockings.

NATALIE PORTMAN IN SLEEK LACE

Evening Bags

TWINKLE, TWINKLE: HERE ARE YOUR LITTLE STARS. YOU NEED AT LEAST TWO

WRISTLET

WEAR IT WELL
Part bracelet, part bag, with its elaborate decoration and delicate handles. And it frees your hands to hold your drink. Perfection.

CHAIN

WEAR IT WELL
This hands-free style can be vintage in shape or sculptural and modern. Elegant with an evening suit, less ideal with a strapless dress.

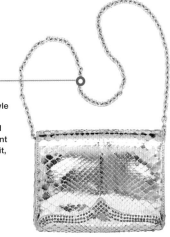

CLUTCH

WEAR IT WELL
A structured, geometric shape will make a modern statement. Pair with razor-sharp silhouettes like pencil skirts and brocade jackets.

SATIN CLUTCH

WEAR IT WELL
How it beckons to be held, or tucked under your arm. The dressier the occasion, the more appropriate a clutch.

looks we love

VINTAGE FRAME

WEAR IT WELL
Frame bags are anything but dowdy. Their retro appeal can work with the most formal clothes, or jeans and a sweet little jacket.

MINAUDIERE

WEAR IT WELL
These small, hard-framed, jewel-encrusted bags were popularized by Cartier (and recently, designer Judith Leiber) and have a serious sense of whimsy.

EMMY ROSSUM CARRIES A SILVERY CLUTCH

Evening Shoes

CLICK YOUR HEELS; THESE EVENING SLIPPERS WILL TAKE YOU PLACES

SATIN

WEAR THEM WELL
Crystal-adorned satin shoes are no-holds-barred dressy. An updated way to wear them is in a contrasting color to your dress.

SLIDES

WEAR THEM WELL
This shoe's gotta fit, since nothing beyond gravity is holding it on. (Better for dinner than dancing.) Since it's so open, they're real leg lengtheners.

BLACK

WEAR THEM WELL
As in, not-so-basic black. Elegant with the LBD (and more unexpected than classic pumps), they also work with jeans and a sexy black top.

METALLIC STRAPPY

WEAR THEM WELL
Make gold or silver part of your party palette. In general, gold shoes are a match for earth-toned clothes. Silver complements pastels.

ANKLE-STRAPS

WEAR THEM WELL
Sexy with a slightly retro vibe, this style is best shown off with skirts. But beware: The line they create around the ankle cuts off leg length.

VELVET

WEAR THEM WELL
A little richness of fabric goes a long way. Lustrous silk or satin clothes will look best with your plush shoes.

PEEP-TOE PUMPS

WEAR THEM WELL
The classic stiletto gets cheekier for evening in an animal print and open toe. Wear with a femme fatale suit, cigarette pants or a pencil skirt.

SLINGBACKS

WEAR THEM WELL
The shape is a real leg lengthener with its thin-sole heel, pointed toe and semi-open back. Obvious jewels make a shoe strictly for night.

Great Evening Looks

PUTTIN' ON THE GLITZ FOR NIGHTTIME AFFAIRS

OPEN HOUSE
Add a velvet jacket and an embellished bag to work staples like wool trousers and you'll look festive but relaxed—perfect for a house party.

FORMAL
Sure, long dresses or skirts fit the code, but shorter dresses can work too in a rich fabric (this one's silk chiffon) and one-of-a-kind details.

COCKTAIL PARTY
Deep jewel tones add wearable color. Mismatched shoes and bag look current. A chunky necklace is better than pearls with a strapless dress.

OFFICE PARTY
Elegant pants plus a knockout top will be more comfortable than a hot little number. Sub an evening bag and shoes before you head out.

3

4

HOLIDAY DINNER
Wide silk pants (try drawstring pajama styles too) are flattering and comfy as you eat. A keyhole top offers sex appeal for smaller busts.

NEW YEAR'S EVE
When glitter is an option, metallics plus white make a cool combination. A flowing skirt lets you dance; the short jacket adds balance.

5

6

ROMANTIC DINNER
Red always has impact,
especially on a date. If
your coloring is more cool,
try a burgundy, or shades
with a purple base.

7

PARTY-HOPPING
Black evening pants, a
structured camisole
and elegant extras can
take you from a charity
auction to a friend's
cocktail party.

8

CHAPTER 4

Spring/Summer Wardrobe

◯ **LIGHTEN UP** When it comes to fashion, you may suffer from seasonal affective disorder. If you feel a bit tepid on warm-weather dressing (or a bit too reliant on hum-drum khakis and a tired T), this chapter might provide a cure. We'll show you how to boost your spring/summer basics to be every bit as versatile and enduring as your fall staples (a grownup trenchcoat, dynamite cropped pants, a snappy pair of shorts), and how to build outfits you love, head to toe, T to espadrille.

Capsule Wardrobe

Fun and fundamentals come together in your spring/summer pieces. Have a white T-shirt you love? The wear-everywhere sundress?

EXPRESS YOURSELF Color, prints, beads, straw, seashells on our shoes. Spring and summer are about cutting loose and being more spontaneous with our clothes—as much, that is, as our lives let us, since we still need to look appropriate for work, or the PTA meeting, or weddings, weddings, weddings. Your basics, then, need to be flexible—as hardworking as your fall trousers and white shirts but open to the possibility of sudden change—and last-minute beach weekends. Here, a few of our favorite mix-and-match pieces.

 ✓ white t-shirt

 ✓ trench

 ✓ camisole

 ✓ straw bag

 ✓ cotton shorts

 ✓ canvas tote

 ✓ khaki pants

 ✓ thong sandals

 ✓ cotton skirt

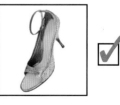 ✓ open-toe work shoe

 ✓ sundress

 ✓ swimsuit

 ✓ cotton cardigan

 ✓ beach cover-up

Lightweight Coats

THE BEST WAYS TO COVER UP FOR RAIN OR AN EVENING CHILL

TRENCH

WHAT WE LOVE
Appropriated by American women around WWII, the style ranks today as the go-everywhere icon.
WEAR IT WELL
Invest in waterproof, wrinkle-resistant fabric; banish baggy or voluminous versions.

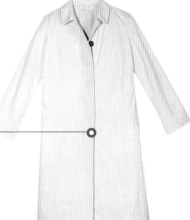

BALMACAAN

WHAT WE LOVE
It has menswear appeal (with or without raglan sleeves) and a no-fuss fit.
WEAR IT WELL
The shape looks best with trim pants and won't work as well with skirts and dresses.

DOUBLE-BREASTED

WHAT WE LOVE
With the durable appeal of the peacoat, plus length, it goes casual or to work.
WEAR IT WELL
Better for taller women; petites will want single-breasted shapes.

COLOR

WHAT WE LOVE
For a new take on the classic trench, try red, chartreuse or powder blue.
WEAR IT WELL
Avoid wrinkles with cotton blended with polyester or nylon, or go for a wool-microfiber-spandex mix.

looks we love

SHORT

WHAT WE LOVE
If you drive a lot, you'll appreciate a shorter length that sits at hips.

WEAR IT WELL
Sleeves should cover wrist bones; any back flaps should easily fall closed and lie flat.

DRESSY

WHAT WE LOVE
With its half-dress, half-coat appeal, wear a simple sheath underneath and be formally attired.

WEAR IT WELL
Look for a rich, glittery fabric like brocade and a lining that doesn't pull or buckle.

LUCY LIU WEARS A CLASSIC TRENCH

Jackets and Sweaters

OVER EASY? SUMMER CARDIGANS, SPRING FLORALS AND ANYTIME DENIM

CARDIGAN

WHAT WE LOVE
Go for a lightweight, belted version. Feminine details like scalloped edges will complement soft skirts.

WEAR IT WELL
Teal, orange or red all add life to your summer whites and khakis.

BLAZER

WHAT WE LOVE
With its nipped-in waist and three-button front, you can wear one with nothing underneath.

WEAR IT WELL
Any shift in pattern at the seams should be a deliberate detail, not the result of sloppy sewing.

FEMININE

WHAT WE LOVE
A floral that's sweet but packs some color punch will enliven work staples without looking dated.

WEAR IT WELL
This very fitted shape looks best either fully buttoned or not at all.

DENIM

WHAT WE LOVE
A fitted shape in soft denim (blue or white) will top off anything from a sundress to Bermudas.

WEAR IT WELL
Toss out older styles that have a boxy fit or hit lower than hip level.

looks we love

EMBELLISHED

WHAT WE LOVE
No longer just for night, it covers a summer dress or works with white jeans and gold heels.

WEAR IT WELL
Glitz at the neck and cuffs means you can skip a necklace and bracelet.

SPORTY

WHAT WE LOVE
These structured styles have rakish charm and instant impact.

WEAR IT WELL
Pair this sporty look, or its cousin, the hoodie, with cropped pants and flat leather sneaks for laid-back chic.

JOY BRYANT IN A CASUAL TUXEDO JACKET

One Sweater, Two Ways

PLAYING UP THE ELEGANT SIDE OF THE SIMPLE COTTON CARDIGAN

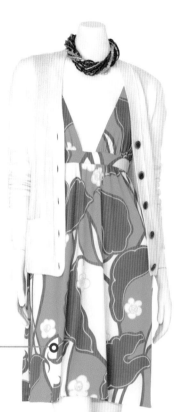

1 →

SUMMER CHILL
Watch it bring sophistication to the sleeveless sundress; the mix of silhouettes works in part because necklines match.

2 →

EASY ELEGANCE
Skip all-black for summer; subbing bold whites, in a crisp sweater and smart leather bag, looks much more fresh.

One Jacket, Two Ways

A CLEVER SHAPE IN A RELIABLE NEUTRAL CAN EXPAND YOUR OPTIONS

1 →

URBAN SAFARI
It's current and cool to layer shirts with different sleeve lengths, especially when the contrast looks deliberate.

2 →

MODERN COUNTRY
The irresistible white dress becomes a lot more wearable with the addition of the tailored but feminine little jacket.

Tops

SHAPES AND STYLES FOR EVERY BODY AND EVERY OCCASION

WHITE T

WHAT WE LOVE
It gives all-American cool to everything from boyfriend jeans to circle skirts.

WEAR IT WELL
Replace seasonally so they stay fresh. Buy high-quality cotton since whites show more imperfections than darks.

TANK

WHAT WE LOVE
The racerback makes a sporty update; closely placed straps are ideal for narrow shoulders.

WEAR IT WELL
If you're busty, avoid all but the most narrow ribbing on any cotton tank or T.

HALTER

WHAT WE LOVE
The shoulder-barer instantly jazzes up everything from shorts to denim skirts.

WEAR IT WELL
Cutouts and ruffles at the bust can be ideal for flattering smaller chests.

CAP-SLEEVE

WHAT WE LOVE
A lacy blouse has lots of finish, perfect for wearing solo on a warm night.

WEAR IT WELL
It's more bra-friendly than a camisole, but check for any show-through given the light fabric.

looks we love

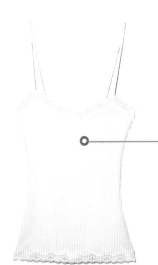

CAMISOLE

WHAT WE LOVE
Silk and lace add feminine
charm when worn under
a serious suit jacket.

WEAR IT WELL
A nude strapless bra
will work best under
white silk; or try layering
a couple of camis.

DRESSY TANK

WHAT WE LOVE
Casual shape (and
bra-friendly straps) plus
sequins add up to
downtown cool.

WEAR IT WELL
Short-waisted? Wear
untucked at your hip. Pair
with white jeans for a
nighttime look.

REBECCA ROMIJN IN LAYERED CAMIS

One Shirt, Four Ways

A LITTLE STARCH, A LOT OF PRESENCE—WITH EVERYTHING FROM A MINI TO A SUIT

1 →

BIG NIGHT
Paging Sharon Stone: Tuck into a high-waisted full silk skirt and you're ready for a fancy cocktail affair.

2 →

PLAY DATE
Darn, I forgot my croquet mallet. Achieve sporty chic appeal with a vest and mini.

3 →

SUBURBAN RESORT
White on white: One of
the chicest looks we
know. A silk sash and
sandals keep it relaxed.

4 →

BUSINESS COOL
Simplicity works
when your spring suit
and white shirt fit this
well. Your only call
now: Collar in or out?

Your T-Shirt Options

THERE'S A WORLD OF DIFFERENCE WITHIN THIS LIMITED UNIVERSE

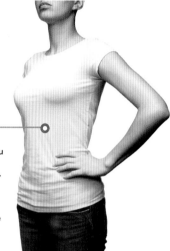

CREWNECK

WHAT WE LOVE
It's casual and classic. If you find the ideal fit, sleeve length and fabric, buy three.
WEAR IT WELL
Finishing is key; stitching should be delicate, and the neckline and hem should lie flat and feel seamless.

CAP SLEEVE

WHAT WE LOVE
This angled sleeve can broaden shoulders but requires toned upper arms.
WEAR IT WELL
Wear a seamless bra with a fitted T. If rolls of flesh show, seek thicker shirt fabric or a different bra.

V-NECK

WHAT WE LOVE
The wide, deep neck gives it a sexy look. Better than a crew for large busts.
WEAR IT WELL
The shoulder seam should sit at the widest part of your natural shoulder.

FINE GAUGE

WHAT WE LOVE
Tissue-thin, highly processed cotton adds a whole new level of luxury to the T.
WEAR IT WELL
Crewneck styles beg to be layered. Pair unexpected hues.

SCOOPNECK

WHAT WE LOVE
It's a great match with flowing skirts, and the scoop helps balance wider hips.

WEAR IT WELL
Avoid unfitted, wide sleeves or those that hit at the center of your bicep.

LONG SLEEVE

WHAT WE LOVE
Sophisticated and flattering for all, especially with a little scoopneck.

WEAR IT WELL
To wear under a suit, choose a fine cotton fabric or blends with Lycra, nylon or rayon.

NICOLE RICHIE GLOWS IN A WHITE TANK

Dresses

WHAT COULD BE EASIER? FIND YOUR FLATTERER, ZIP UP AND GO

FLUTTERY

WHAT WE LOVE
The sheer version of this flattering sleeve gives coverage but keeps you cool.

WEAR IT WELL
A dress with reined-in flow won't make you feel like a whirling dervish.

HALTER

WHAT WE LOVE
The overall cut and gorgeous tie detail help flatter narrow shoulders.

WEAR IT WELL
The slightly longer skirt length and volume would best be balanced with a thicker heel.

SUNDRESS

WHAT WE LOVE
It says summer is here. A waist-emphasizing cut with fullness in the skirt is great for a pear shape.

WEAR IT WELL
Look for distinctive, grown-up prints and skip tiny, girlish florals that can look too young.

STRAPLESS

WHAT WE LOVE
It speaks to our inner prep, works in the heat, and disguises small busts with stripes.

WEAR IT WELL
But does it stay up? Raise arms, twist and check for any gap up top when you lean forward.

looks we love

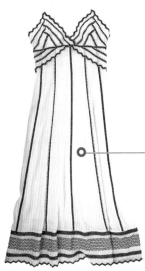

EMPIRE

WHAT WE LOVE
The high waist plus narrow silhouette make this one ideal for petites.
WEAR IT WELL
It looks best if your frame (and bra choice) work with spaghetti straps.

SHIRTDRESS

WHAT WE LOVE
The fuller shape can be more forgiving than straighter styles.
WEAR IT WELL
Pumps have the right vibe, but strappy sandals tend to lengthen legs more.

KERI RUSSELL IN A FIFTIES-STYLE DRESS

Skirts

ONE FOR EVERY MOOD, FROM FREEWHEELING CARGO TO FLIRTY FULL

A-LINE

WHAT WE LOVE
That gentle flare plus a kicky print: Just add espadrilles and a solid T.

WEAR IT WELL
Avoid oversize prints, like large florals, if you're large or hippy.

PLEATED

WHAT WE LOVE
Sewn-down pleats at the top and gradual fullness at the bottom are friendly to hourglass shapes.

WEAR IT WELL
All but the skinniest legs need a little heel with a fuller skirt; try a mid-height peep-toe.

TIERED

WHAT WE LOVE
Lots of swing, with weekend and travel appeal.

WEAR IT WELL
Take the length a bit lower than midcalf to flatter legs.

STRAIGHT

WHAT WE LOVE
For a cutting-edge take, pair a shiny fabric with a cotton tank and heels.

WEAR IT WELL
If a small waist and larger hips are creating a gap up top, have a tailor add darts.

CARGO

WHAT WE LOVE
As much throw-on-and-go appeal as your khakis, but cooler than pants for the summer.

WEAR IT WELL
Pockets draw the eye to where they are placed; look for some that are as flat as these.

MINI

WHAT WE LOVE
Vertical stripes make this strip of fabric as flattering as it can be. Buckles help adjust the fit.

WEAR IT WELL
Wear with flats or thongs; heels with a mini equals too much with too little.

KRISTIN DAVIS IN BREEZY BLACK AND WHITE

One Dress, Two Ways

PERFECT SUMMER STRAPLESS SEEKS LIFE BEYOND GARDEN PARTY

1 →

BODICE GRIPPER
A little cardigan always
works over a sundress,
but for the young and
fashion-forward, a
snug T-shirt under-
neath adds edge.

2 →

WELCOME CONTRAST
You just discovered a
great match for your
vintage-inspired cropped
jacket and a way to wear
strapless to work.

One Skirt, Two Ways

A PRETTY PRINT GOES SPORTY OR ROMANTIC IN TWO EASY SHIFTS

1 →

SUMMER BREEZE
Play against type by combining the skirt's feminine appeal with a more athletic tank.

2 →

NOVEL ROMANCE
The skirt's mood is mirrored in a lacy top and tissue-weight cardigan.

Shorts and Pants

LONG, FULL, TRIM, SHORT: FIND YOUR MOST USEFUL STYLES

SHORT SHORTS

WHAT WE LOVE
It has that forties sexpot thing, which you can update by wearing with a smart tailored jacket and heels.

WEAR THEM WELL
The pleats, the length, the cuffs—they're cute but not for all shapes, sizes and ages.

LONG SHORTS

WHAT WE LOVE
The trim fit dresses up or down easily, and the length flatters most legs and heights.

WEAR THEM WELL
Take the footwear up a notch; try with strappy or crisscross heels.

CROPPED

WHAT WE LOVE
Tailored takes never look dated and work for women of all heights.

WEAR THEM WELL
Shorter pants can sometimes make legs look short; avoid cuffs if you're petite.

DRAWSTRING

WHAT WE LOVE
Ease, please. Comfortably chic for a Saturday picnic or a walk on the beach.

WEAR THEM WELL
Don't tuck shirts in. A fitted cami or T worn on the outside will cover the drawstring and add shape.

KHAKIS

WHAT WE LOVE
Need we say...versatility?
Splurge on professional
pressing if you'll wear
them to work.
WEAR THEM WELL
The slightly fuller leg is
flattering; a wide waist-
band can help hold in a
stomach.

WHITE JEANS

WHAT WE LOVE
They're as endlessly
wearable as blue jeans
but crisper for summer.
WEAR THEM WELL
Check for any show-
through with pockets.
A flare at the hem can
help balance hips.

EVE WORKS A PAIR OF CROPPED PANTS

Shorts, Three Ways

SHORTS HAVE A WHOLE NEW ATTITUDE. FEEL FREE TO EXPERIMENT

1 →

NEO PREP
The new Bermudas are trim and polished with a flat front. Kick 'em up a notch with ankle-straps (if your legs can handle more of a spotlight).

2 →

MIAMI NICE
A long camisole looks perfectly chic with shorts in a dressy, dark fabric. Complete with clutch and slides.

3 →

ALL-DAY URBAN
A sporty jacket plus a print T means signature cool. Dressy? Casual? Keep blurring the line and add a heel.

CHARLIZE THERON DOES SHORTS RIGHT

Swimsuits

COME ON, YOU CAN DO IT. WE MAKE IT EASY TO SUIT YOURSELF

IF YOU'VE BEEN TREADING WATER with a good enough swimsuit, it's time to make more of a splash. With all the style variety and sizing options out there now, you owe it to yourself to take the cannonball approach to this year's pick. Try on the tanks and maillots you know have worked for you in the past, but bring a few new looks into the dressing room too. To help you wade in, we've outlined the shapes and styles to look for now, with advice on finding your own minor miracle worker. Goodbye angst, hello poolside.

A LITTLE ADVICE FOR THAT PRE-SUMMER PILGRIMAGE TO THE RACKS

1 **GIVE IT TIME** You need to be prepared to try on a lot of bikinis. That means shopping on a day you aren't rushed (or hungry, cranky and—especially—self-loathing) and well in advance of your flight to Tahiti.

2 **START BIG** Start with a number two clicks up from your dress size; suits simply tend to run small. But you also need to accept that some cuts will never work for you no matter what the size. "And remember, going up in size simply to get more coverage will throw off the proportion," says swimwear designer Malia Mills. Everything will look a little big and a little wrinkly.

3 **READ LABELS** The denser the fabric, and the more Lycra involved, the more control a suit will offer. Just be sure there's no sausage effect at the leg openings or around the bust from a suit with too much control for you.

4 **SURPRISE YOURSELF** Strike a balance between understanding what looks good on your figure and being open to trying on new styles. Abandoning preconceived notions about the exact style you want to buy will make the shopping trip a lot more zen.

5 **AFTER CUT AND FIT, CONSIDER COLOR** If you're pale, a black, dark brown or navy suit may complement your skin tone better than white or pastels. And while metallic suits offer style points, matte fabrics are almost always more slimming than shiny ones.

Basic Suit Shapes

THERE'S ONE FOR EVERY BODY; CONSIDER CUT AND COVERAGE

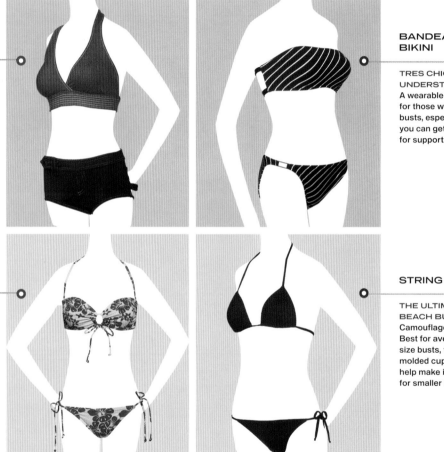

BOY SHORTS

**SEX APPEAL WITH
A SPORTY SIDE**
The banded halter
and its wider straps
give support for larger
busts, while the
darker briefs scale
down hips.

**BANDEAU
BIKINI**

**TRES CHIC, IN AN
UNDERSTATED WAY**
A wearable shape
for those with bigger
busts, especially if
you can get extra Lycra
for support.

**KEYHOLE
BANDEAU**

**SO CUTE AND
HELPS A LITTLE
(BUST) GO A
LONG WAY**
While plainer ban-
deaus often appear
to flatten the chest,
a style like this—with
a keyhole, front
ruching and interior
boning—can enhance.

STRING

**THE ULTIMATE
BEACH BUDDY**
Camouflage? No.
Best for average-
size busts, though
molded cups can
help make it work
for smaller chests.

TANKINI

LAID-BACK CHIC
Comfortably fits
longer-than-average
torsos but won't
offer control
or shaping for
straighter or
fuller waists.

SHIRT BIKINI

**SASSY AND
HIGHLY INDIVIDUAL**
A tiny bikini bottom
elongates the waist,
which is flattering
unless you're long-
waisted to start.
The fuller top
balances hips.

ONE-PIECE
PLUNGE

**GROWN-UP
COME-HITHER**
Distracts from wider
hips, and works for
smaller chests. And
high necks tend to
broaden shoulders,
slim waists.

ONE-PIECE
TANK

EASY DOES IT
A gentle V up top is
universally flattering;
and slightly higher-
cut legs can down-
play larger thighs.

Play Up Your Figure

FLAWS? WHAT FLAWS? MORE TRICKS THAT FLATTER

1 →

SHIRRED TORSO
WORKS FOR
THICKER WAISTS
Gathered fabric
at the midsection
reduces the
appearance of
bulges and creates
the illusion of a
defined waist. Seek
similar aid from
matte fabrics,
draped waists,
diagonal stripes
and side cutouts.

2 →

LIVELY PRINT
WORKS FOR
ALLOVER
SLIMMING
Some patterns are
more slimming than
others, but in
general one that
is big, bold and has
a lot of movement
will offer distraction
from body flaws.
A print with a dark
background is
also safe.

3 →

RUFFLED BIKINI
WORKS FOR
BOYISH FIGURES
Even little ruffles
can make you look
bigger. Up top—
especially in look-
at-me white—this
translates as a boost
for smaller chests.
Just make sure the
suit is double-lined,
not see-through.

4 →

TWO-TONE BIKINI
WORKS FOR
PEAR SHAPES
Any suit with a
darker bottom and
lighter top will bring
the eye up instead
of down. A twist-
front bandeau
and angled straps
also help frame
and create cleavage
for those smaller
up top.

Bags

BET YOU CAN'T CHOOSE JUST ONE. NOR SHOULD YOU

BUCKLE

WEAR IT WELL
For errands or lighter days at the office you'll appreciate the organization of a structured bag with lots of pockets, inside and out.

WORK TOTE

WEAR IT WELL
Sure, your look loosens up a bit in spring, but a work bag still needs to look tidy and smart. Opt for leather trim and a subtle design.

CLUTCH

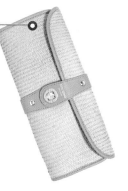

WEAR IT WELL
It's a stylish update to the small shoulder bag. Make sure it will hold your cell phone, lipstick, wallet and keys.

CANVAS

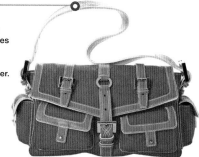

WEAR IT WELL
A fabric day bag in a practical shape scores for worry-free chic. And it's more lightweight than all-leather.

looks we love

STRAW

WEAR IT WELL
Whether in a classic basket or tote, straw just feels right for summer. Choose a closed top or interior zipped pockets for security.

BEACH TOTE

WEAR IT WELL
Think roomy, colorful and hardy. Look for a tightly woven straw or plastic and a lining you can wipe clean after a day in the sand.

UMA THURMAN WITH A CLASSIC LOGO BAG

Shoes

CHIC PICKS TO TAKE YOU TO THE PARK, BEACH OR OFFICE

CRISS-CROSS

WEAR THEM WELL
It's a glam look that wakes up white pants or khakis and emphasizes the shape of the foot and ankle.

ESPADRILLES

WEAR THEM WELL
The cute classic with the wearable wedge heel. Slip on with shorts, denim or floral skirts, or crops. Probably not for work.

FLATS

WEAR THEM WELL
Dress them with narrow or cropped pants, or long or short skirts. With knee-length skirts they can look dowdy.

PEEP-TOE FLATS

WEAR THEM WELL
An open toe creates a flat/sandal hybrid that works with everything from a floral dress to jeans. Large feet will look better in a heel.

THONGS

It's the versatile, grown-up flip-flop that's seriously packable. Be patient and find a pair that doesn't rub between toes.

SLINGBACKS

WEAR THEM WELL
The sexy shape flatters thick ankles or heavy calves. But even closed-toe versions shouldn't be worn with stockings.

SLIDES

WEAR THEM WELL
This graceful style goes best with all-black or all-white clothing. Pairing with graphic black-and-white would be too much.

EMBELLISHED THONGS

WEAR THEM WELL
Minimal height and a lot of detail. The style is an ideal partner with full skirts that share their flirty and feminine appeal.

Great Looks for Work

HOW THOSE ESSENTIAL SHAPES AND STYLES MIX AND MATCH FOR THE OFFICE

EASY SELL
Find a skirt with a creative but tailored shape and you won't have to work hard to bring it to life; striped pumps optional.

FISCAL REPORT
You realize the colorful, print jacket wasn't such a splurge when it so effortlessly wakes up your basic work pants.

TUESDAY AFTERNOON
Casual suit pants feel right in the heat. So do the latest white pumps; but keep them nice, not nursey, with open toes or cutouts.

3

GRAPHICS DEPARTMENT
Très chic: black and white combined with simple geometric shapes and shots of candy red.

4

YOUTHFUL AMBITION
Get away with denim for
work by choosing a skirt
with a dark wash and
adding tasteful, cheerful
accents around it.

DIVERSITY TRAINING
Don't be afraid to blend
stripes with a print
if the pieces are in the
same color family.
Matching bag and shoes
add extra continuity.

SUBTLE APPROACH
It only takes a small shot of color to bring neutrals to life. Try sophisticated hues like lime, chartreuse or tangerine.

7

CASUAL FRIDAY
Start with trouser jeans, then add polish: bow-front flats and a preppy bag, plus the timeless blouse-under-shirt combo.

8

Great Looks for Weekend

TRY YOUR OWN TAKE ON THESE SPIRITED, HEAD-TO-TOE ENSEMBLES

PARK PICNIC
Did we forget to put a tunic
on your list of must-have
shirts? Shame on us. They're
easy to wear and perfect
with the simplest jeans.

BEACH TRIP
Ideal to pack for the
weekend: A crinkle skirt
never looks wrinkled,
and a white tank goes
with everything.

PLAY DATE
Why be dull? Even your most casual shorts deserve a little styling; add a cute cotton voile halter, a ribbon belt and retro seventies sandals.

CANNES DO
Nautical navy and white plus the gamine appeal of cropped jeans is timelessly chic. If flats don't flatter, try wedges.

3

4

BOHEMIAN BIT
An updater that should graduate to basic: the lightweight cotton bolero that instantly completes Bermudas and a T.

5

SUNNY-SIDE UP
A trick to trying out big beads? Match them to your top and they'll feel (slightly) less bold.

6

SPA CHECK-IN
Look and feel zen with pants and a T that imitate the cut of yoga gear. An Eastern-inspired cotton jacket pulls it together.

7

HIPPIE CHIC
A tunic dress with a high waist combines laid-back appeal with wearability. Don't be afraid of a little contrast with your shoes and bag.

8

Great Looks for Evening

PULLED-TOGETHER STYLE FOR WHATEVER EVENTS THE SEASON HOLDS

JUNE WEDDING
Break free from black
and fulfill any number of
dress codes in a long
and sensuous silk dress.

WITH THE BAND
Can you mix gold and
silver? Colored stones?
Sure, if you're combin-
ing cheeky accents and
the rest of your outfit
has unified cool.

GRADUATION
Black and white never
fails for easy elegance,
but adding the spring
occasion coat in a con-
trasting color or print
sets you apart.

40TH BIRTHDAY
Yellow has resurfaced as
an unexpected knockout
for evening. If you're in
doubt about the go-to
shoe, try a metallic.

CELEBRATION BRUNCH
Part shrug, part sweater, a little cashmere topper makes ultrafeminine dresses (like sweet white lace) more versatile.

NIGHTCLUB
Break down this dance look and, along with sequins, you'll find true evening basics: wide-leg silk pants and wear-forever gold bangles.

5°

6°

CATERED COCKTAILS
Go strapless. And know a fuller cut in a heavier fabric, such as cotton, will hide flaws better than a straight-and-slinky tube.

7

BIG DINNER
In a pantsuit, all-white is all about power and confidence. But for full authority see a tailor for any fit tweaks.

8

CHAPTER 5

Beyond Basics

LINGERIE, JEWELRY, TRAVEL Under the theme of little things that mean a lot, let's first consider your lingerie. Are you the type who never met a lacy camisole you didn't love, or more of a cotton panties-and-forget-about-it minimalist? Either way, it bears repeating that you can't neglect the lingerie fundamentals; they really can make or break your look (form-fitting Ts with crinkly bras: enough said). Find your list of essential underpinnings here, then jump to the fun stuff: your jewelry collection. From classic investment pieces to the latest trends, we're betting you'll be tempted to try something new. Our final beyond-basics topic—travel—challenges you to bring it all together, and take it on the road.

Lingerie

WHAT YOU NEED TO WEAR UNDERNEATH IT ALL

HIDDEN ASSETS If lingerie is always last on your shopping list, it may be time to move these fundamentals up a notch or two. After all, your carefully considered clothes will never look quite right without the proper underpinnings. (And who doesn't get a charge out of a beautiful new camisole?) So don't skimp. Start with your bras and take the time to find the shapes you need in the perfect size for you. (Our first pointer? Have a pro in the lingerie department officially size you up.) Your form-hugging Ts and strapless shifts will thank you.

HAVING A FIT? SOLUTIONS TO COMMON BRA ISSUES

PROBLEM: THE BACK RIDES UP Try tightening the hook or loosening the straps. If that doesn't work, go down a size. If you see rolls of flesh above the back strap, the band (as opposed to the cup) size may be too small.

PROBLEM: FALL-DOWN STRAPS If adjusting them fails, try going down a size. Bra straps are at the correct length if your bra is level across the back and not too tight when using the middle hooks. The slope of your shoulder could be the problem; in that case, a T-back shape might work best.

PROBLEM: THE CUPS ARE WRINKLY If it's a new bra, try getting into it this way: Lean over, jiggle a bit, and let your breasts "fall" into the cups. If that doesn't fix the creasing, you may need to go down one band size.

4

PROBLEM: FRONT GAP The center front of a bra should be flush against your sternum. If it's not, the bra may be too small or the wrong style for you.

5

PROBLEM: SPILLAGE If you're busting out at the sides or over the top of the cups, you may need a larger cup size or a shape with more coverage on the sides and top.

Bra Shapes

BEFORE MORNING-OF PANIC HITS, FIND THE SHAPES YOU'LL NEED

NO UNDERWIRE

WHAT IT IS
An everyday bra with
no padding or wiring;
the thick band below
your bust supports.
LOOK FOR
Wider straps give
more support; thick
or nylon-and-spandex
cups look smooth.

CONTOUR

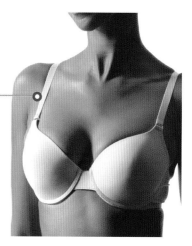

WHAT IT IS
A seamless bra with
flexible underwire.
Foam linings help
under clingy tops.
LOOK FOR
Underwire channels
that are fully cush-
ioned; they'll be more
comfortable.

PUSH-UP

WHAT IT IS
Designed with molded,
slightly angled cups
to lift and enhance
cleavage.
LOOK FOR
Underwire if you're a
B cup or bigger; a
wireless, lightly lined
cup if you're an A.

BUST MINIMIZER

WHAT IT IS
Reduces the size of
breasts by about one
cup size.
LOOK FOR
A full, round cup for
even distribution of
the breasts. Make sure
straps fit securely.

BUST ENHANCER

WHAT IT IS
The cut helps push the bust upward; the fabric amplifies and sculpts.

LOOK FOR
Lined cups or add-in padding called cookies. Make sure cups fit flat on breasts.

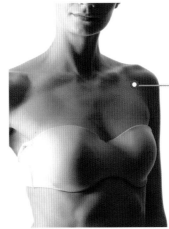

CONVERTIBLE

WHAT IT IS
A bra that can be worn strapless, halter, crisscross or over one or both shoulders.

LOOK FOR
Stretch foam cups. If strapless bra slips, go down a band size or up a cup size.

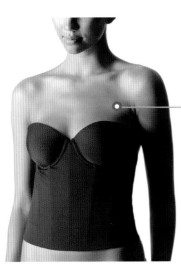

LOW BACK

WHAT IT IS
Perfect for tight, strapless looks, it gets its support from the waist.

LOOK FOR
A close fit at mid section that still lets you bend, twist and easily raise arms.

SPORTS

WHAT IT IS
A full-coverage bra in moisture-wicking fabric that gives enough support for workouts.

LOOK FOR
Underwire styles if you're a C cup or above, and ample fabric on the sides for everyone.

Panties, Body Shapers

GET A LITTLE WAIST MANAGEMENT AND AVOID VISIBLE PANTY LINES

THONG

WHAT IT IS
It's the ultimate in no panty-line, but you trade any cover or shaping in the rear.
LOOK FOR
A back strip that's soft enough to feel good hours later.

BRIEF

WHAT IT IS
A wider-cut panty with more front and rear coverage; it's sexier with details like lace cutouts or mesh fabric.
LOOK FOR
A cotton blend will retain its shape when washed repeatedly.

SHAPER SLIP

WORKS UNDER
The clingy dress or sexy skirt and camisole.
LOOK FOR
Seamless nylon-spandex fabric. Make sure the hem doesn't ride up and check that there's no see-through with lighter fabrics.

BODYSUIT

WORKS UNDER
Anything from stretchy pants to formfitting knits.
LOOK FOR
The bra style and strap width should match your top. Built-in bras with underwire give more support.

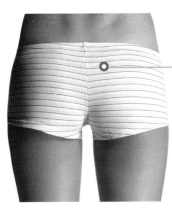

BOY SHORT

WHAT IT IS
An up-and-comer in the panty world that can look surprisingly free of panty lines.
LOOK FOR
Lacy versions with angled leg openings make this style more sexy than sporty.

BIKINI

WHAT IT IS
Before thongs and boy shorts, we had these sweet nothings, in string or basic styles.
LOOK FOR
No gap between the side string and rear fabric.

BIKE SHORTS

WORKS UNDER
Pencil skirts or tough-to-wear bias cuts.
LOOK FOR
With a high stretch content, make sure nothing digs into your skin and you don't have spillover at the waist.

THIGH/WAIST SLIMMER

WORKS UNDER
Belted dresses or gowns, or fashionable high-waist trousers.
LOOK FOR
Make sure construction is seamless on tummy panels, which add control at waist.

Jewelry Wardrobe

DON'T FORGET THESE IMPORTANT FINISHING TOUCHES

ALL THAT GLITTERS From the most personal keepsakes to the trendiest baubles and beads, our jewelry says a lot about us—and completes a great many looks. Want to build your collection? We've outlined the classics as well as of-the-minute updaters, and culled the best advice for how to wear your chains, bangles and chandeliers well.

HOW TO ADD SOME SHINE AND KNOW WHICH PIECES SUIT YOU BEST

1 **AVOID MATCHY-MATCHY** Yes, you want your pieces to complement each other and be of the same mood and level of formality. But combining is now more of a personal statement and less about following the law of similars.

2 **MAKE A SINGLE STATEMENT** In general the more sparkle in your clothes, the less you need in your jewelry. One outsize piece is often enough, and you should always watch the proximity of big or bold pieces. Chandeliers and a cuff bracelet can work together, but chandeliers with a chunky necklace are too much, too close.

3 **CONSIDER THE SHAPE OF YOUR FACE** If your face is round, then round earrings (especially large ones that sit on the lobe) will only make cheeks look more full. Instead, choose a dangling or drop earring. Square faces look best with small, oval or oblong earrings; oval faces can wear just about any earring.

4 **MAKE YOUR NECKLACE WORK FOR YOUR NECK** Long styles (chains, lariats, etc.) flatter those with short necks, broad shoulders or short torsos, whereas chokers are best reserved for longer necks.

5 **FIND A RING THAT FLATTERS YOUR FINGERS** The shape of a stone will determine how it looks on your hand. If you're conscious of your fingers being stubby, marquis shapes or ovals give the illusion of length and slenderness.

Jewelry

ESSENTIAL INVESTMENT PIECES

DIAMOND STUDS

WHAT WE LOVE
They light up your face
and are great foils to
more complicated
necklaces and clothes.
WEAR THEM WELL
To save money, choose
studs with a metal
border and smaller stone,
or try a pavé style.

PENDANT NECKLACE

WHAT WE LOVE
A slender chain plus a
hanging charm or gem
is a subtle, personal
accent for both work
and weekend.
WEAR IT WELL
Choose a pendant that
slips over the clasp if
you want to be able to
change it. Opt for
discs, rings, lockets or
organic shapes.

PEARLS

WHAT WE LOVE
You don't have to be a Miss
Porter grad to appreciate
their serious finishing power.
WEAR THEM WELL
Classic styles include single
and double strands; 16 inches
is the most popular length.
A strand made of funky
shapes costs a fraction
of the price of perfectly
round ones.

BANGLES

WHAT WE LOVE
Classic but carefree;
their jingle is part
of their charm.
WEAR THEM WELL
Slender versions
in silver or gold
should be worn in
multiples; wider
versions go solo.

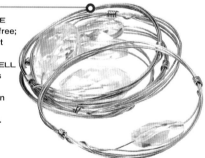

looks we love

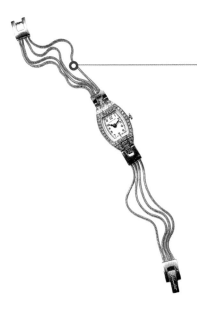

CLASSIC WATCH

WHAT WE LOVE
Clean lines and a simple face make for one piece that can be worn every day.

WEAR IT WELL
Choose a metal or leather strap (black if you wear more black; brown if you favor neutral shades).

ANGELINA JOLIE IN CLASSIC WATCH

EVENING WATCH

WHAT WE LOVE
When you realize your everyday band isn't cutting it with your little black dress, this will do the trick.

WEAR IT WELL
A sprinkle of small diamonds on a steel case is a way to get sparkle for less.

ASHLEY JUDD LAYERS HER PEARLS

Jewelry

THE UPDATERS: PIECES TO HAVE NOW

OVERSIZE COCKTAIL RING

WHAT WE LOVE
Glamorously retro, it adds a big look (and lots of color) without costing a fortune.

WEAR IT WELL
When trying one on, make sure the stone stays upright; you don't want to feel it slipping from side to side.

BIG CUFF

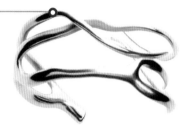

WHAT WE LOVE
The confidence a thick band of gold or silver (or Bakelite, tortoise or filigree) can bestow.

WEAR IT WELL
Pair with modern clothes that have clean lines, from a T-shirt and white jeans to your wool pantsuit.

CHARM NECKLACE

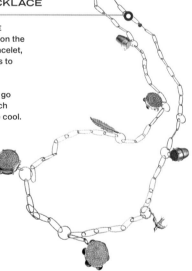

WHAT WE LOVE
The twist it takes on the classic charm bracelet, with endless ways to personalize.

WEAR IT WELL
Don't be afraid to go big and bold; kitsch can be part of the cool.

IMPACT EARRINGS

WHAT WE LOVE
Chandeliers, long linear styles and embellished hoops are your go-to attention grabbers.

WEAR THEM WELL
Make sure they're not too heavy and they flatter your face shape.

looks we love

ETHNIC BRACELETS

WHAT WE LOVE
The pieces you pick up on
your travels (or look like
you did) bring color and
texture to neutral clothes.
WEAR THEM WELL
If you've got an armful of
tribal items, let their rich
appeal take center stage.

JESSICA SIMPSON PULLS OFF BIG BEADS

JEWELED CHAIN

WHAT WE LOVE
The It Necklace has
a long chain strung
with gemstones.
WEAR IT WELL
Stick to one type of
metal and layer with
other chains or
pendants of varied
lengths and sizes.

SARAH JESSICA PARKER IN COSTUME NECKLACE

Travel with Style

OH, THE PLACES YOU'LL GO. BUT WHAT TO WEAR?

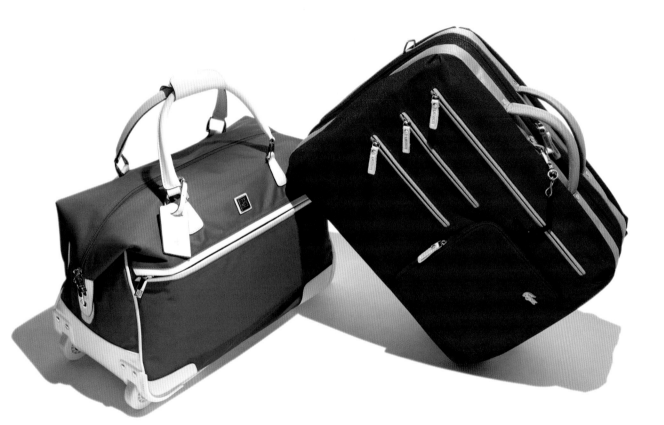

ARE YOU THERE YET? As draining as jet lag, as unsettling as long lines at check-in: that late-night moment when you face the haunting hollow of your empty suitcase and wonder what on earth you should fill it with. Here's how to make the right packing choices (hint: They don't involve sitting on your bag to close it) so you'll have everything you need once the real adventure begins.

HOW MUCH TO BRING Do the math. **FOR AN OVERNIGHT** You need at least two bottoms with two interchangeable tops. Make one set dressy, the other casual. Then throw in a coordinated cardigan, wrap or blazer. **FOR A LONG WEEKEND** Think in terms of mix-and-match pieces. Three tops and two bottoms give you more than five different outfits. If your just-in-case yoga pants can double as pajamas, all the better. **FOR A WEEK OR MORE** Get five days right (plot them from head to toe) and, with the necessary underpinnings, you're prepared for 10. Just rotate tops and bottoms, and change accessories.

1

ALWAYS PACK A CHAMELEON ITEM OR TWO Make sure the item can be worn in different ways. A tunic dress will slip over a bathing suit and, with earrings and the right sandals, look good at night too. A lightweight cardigan can be worn on its own for day or left open with a sexy tank underneath for cocktails.

2

INVEST IN A COLLECTION OF LUXE T-SHIRTS Choose a variety of shapes and sophisticated neutrals. Versions in tissue-weight cottons or cotton-nylon blends are ideal, wrinkle-free wardrobe extenders. You'll wear the cap-sleeve crew under a jacket during the work session, then on its own.

3

SHOES NEED TO WORK EXTRA HARD They're some of the heaviest items in your suitcase, so you don't want to pack too many. You'll want a brown or black option, to match to your wardrobe basics. The best second choice is often a color, like red, or a metallic. Either will pair with black or brown clothes. Updated flats are light (try a peep-toe style) and versatile.

4

DEPARTING IN DRIFTS AND ARRIVING IN THE TROPICS? Make a T your base layer, wear cotton chinos instead of wool, and, if possible, opt for a shell or vest instead of a bulky, hard-to-pack coat. Slip lightweight espadrilles into your carry-on and slip out of your socks and shoes on touchdown.

Packing Essentials

THESE BASICS WILL TAKE YOU JUST ABOUT ANYWHERE

1 **A LONG COAT** It looks sophisticated over smart neutrals like khaki pants and a white shirt and will keep you warm or dry if the weather turns.

2 **A STRUCTURED TOTE AND PURSE** Bring a large tote on the plane and fill it with what you'll need for a day should your luggage be lost. Designate pockets to hold the jewelry you'll remove in security as well as coins or keys emptied from pockets. Your other must-have is a smaller structured purse that will work for day or night.

3 **WEDGES** Flats are current and great for travel, but if you need a little heel wedges can be a good summer option (although they won't slide off as easily in security).

4 **A CARDIGAN-AND-CAMISOLE COMBO** Exact twinset matches are out, but your pieces should work together as well as alone. Cashmere makes an ideal, breathable choice for the cardigan. A cami with a built-in bra is another true wardrobe extender.

5 **A SEASONLESS JERSEY DRESS** If you get a not-too-sexy cut (you'll want a bra-friendly version that hits at the middle of your knee) it will pay off for years as a travel basic. Dress it down with wedges and beads, up with metallic heels and pearls.

Seeing the Sights

OPT FOR COMFORT (NO TIGHT SHOES!) AND VERSATILITY

1   **A LONG SKIRT** You might not wear it much at home, but with a bit of flow it works well in a variety of locales. Plus it shifts easily from day (with a T-shirt and thongs) to evening (with a sleeveless blouse and heels).

2   **A COLORFUL BLOUSE** Get too many neutrals going and you'll find that your well-thought-out wardrobe just looks dull. You need a print or two to liven up your look and draw multiple colors together. That's where a feminine wrap blouse comes in.

3   **TAILORED, STYLISH SHORTS** Scrap the cutoffs or mere khakis. A pair of plaid Bermudas (or a very cropped pair of pants) can be dressed up with heels and a blazer, or go casual with flats and a T.

4   **A PERSONALITY JACKET AND JEANS** Sure, a pair of baggy jeans plus sneakers will mark you as a tourist faster than you can ask for a restroom. But choose a pair in a sophisticated wash and cut (try a dark trouser shape), add a beyond-basic jacket and flats, and you have a go-anywhere look for London or Louisville. And what packs better than denim?

5   **FLAT SHOES** Metallic flats work from beach to cobblestone street. While they won't flatter your leg the way a heel will, their cool-but-casual vibe goes well with a flowy skirt or dressy shorts.

Heading for the Beach

THE TRICK HERE IS PACKING CASUALLY WITHOUT VEERING INTO SLOPPY

1 **A SWIMSUIT AND BEACH COVER-UP** A one-piece suit may work best for the country club, but if you're headed to the islands, consider a bikini (fun to wear and easy to wash and dry). A long shirt (just like a tunic or a simple sundress) can do double duty as a day basic.

2 **A PACKABLE HAT** It's a good alternative to a structured straw hat, and you'll save room in your carry-on. And if it's reversible, even better! All you need now: some oversize sunglasses for extra protection.

3 **DRESSIER THONGS** As opposed to rubber flip-flops, these can take you from poolside to dinner. Look for embellishments like mother-of-pearl or beading to up the style quotient.

4 **A BEACH BAG** Size is an issue: You want it to fit a towel, a book, your sunscreen and more, but be small enough that you can take it to the market as a purse. Look for interior pockets and fabric or leather trim that give it life beyond the dunes.

5 **A COTTON SUNDRESS** Absolutely indispensable. For a richer double life, look for one with a bit more structure and slightly wider straps that accommodate a bra underneath.

Business Class

CLASSICS AND NEUTRAL COLORS WILL KEEP YOU LOOKING SHARP

1   **A BLACK PANTSUIT** It's a stylish basic that dresses up well for night with an embellished tank, long sparkling earrings and strappy heels. A brightly colored blouse or a print scarf is a sure-fire (and lightweight) way to give your suit a new look for day.

2   **BLACK OR BROWN HEELS** Make sure your basic clothing pieces—like a herringbone sheath or cotton blazer and pants—can all be worn with the shoes you've packed.

3   **A CLASSIC TRENCH** This coat looks sharp and will usually accommodate enough layers to insulate against wind, rain and chilly weather. Consider buying one with a detachable wool lining to maximize wearability.

4   **A SHEATH** The right one can handle all kinds of weather, since you can wear it solo or slip a shirt or silk sweater underneath for warmth. For winter a nubbier wool or tweed can offer the right contrast if you want to wear the dress with a sleek suit jacket. What you want to avoid are similar-hued fabrics that look like you tried to match but failed.

5   **A WHITE SHIRT** It slips under your sheath for the meeting and works with your black suit pants for evening. Yes, you want to pack the inimitable white shirt. But to make sure it doesn't wrinkle, place layers of either plastic dry cleaner bags or sheets of tissue between each fold as well as between it and other items in your suitcase.

CHAPTER 6

No-Regrets Shopping

IT STARTS BEFORE YOU LEAVE The most successful shopping trips commence not with double espresso or a bonus at work or brunch with your friends—though those are all nice beginnings too—but with a simple plan. You need one because this happens to everyone at one time or another: Tempted by all the bounty, you suddenly feel your mind glaze over at all the possibilities and become a bit tired by the thought of trying them all on. How to avoid the slump? Just follow our strategy—from setting a budget at home to recognizing quality (and deals!) in the dressing room—and you'll be on your way to better shopping, caffeine-free.

Prep Work

1 **MAKE A LIST** First, go through your closet to determine what you can still wear from last year. Then write down what you need to buy and how much you can spend for each item.

2 **MAP OUT YOUR TRIP** Now, break that list into rational shopping excursions. Give important items like "made-for-me designer jeans" and "break-his-heart dress" a day of their own.

3 **DRESS TO UNDRESS** No belt. No hair-electrifying turtlenecks. No giant parka. Do wear slip-on shoes, the right underpinnings and (for trying on jackets) a close-fitting T.

4 **GIVE YOURSELF TIME** Never shop under the stress of having to buy a dress *today* for a formal event next weekend. Plan ahead and sleep on a purchase if you need to.

Budget Basics

With your wallet, as with your wardrobe, a little common sense goes a long way. Here, a few questions to ask yourself before checkout.

CAN I AFFORD IT? You need to know your yearly clothing budget. "If you're spending more than 20 percent of your after-tax income on clothes, you are out of control," says David Bach, author of *Start Late, Finish Rich*. Ten percent is a better limit.

WHAT'S THE COST PER WEAR? Maybe $1,000 isn't so ridiculous to spend on a coat you'll wear dozens and dozens of times. Maybe $300 is a lot for a dress you'll only wear when you're feeling 19th-century Parisian-street-urchin-ish.

HOW MANY HOURS OF WORK WILL IT TAKE TO PAY FOR IT? If we're talking weeks of behind-the-desk payoff, proceed slowly to the checkout.

COULD I PAY CASH? Your credit card is your business, but most experts recommend you at least be able to pay off the interest on a new purchase.

5 **BRING PROPS** If you'll be trying on evening dresses, for instance, bring heels plus a strapless bra. Pack any necessary items, plus a tiny bottle of water, in an easy-to-access, lightweight tote.

In the Dressing Room

Shop for the here and now

"Never shop thinking, I'll lose a little and it will fit," says Tracey Ross of the Tracey Ross boutique in Los Angeles. "Buy for the moment you're in."

Test drive

Squat and sit in pants. Swing arms front and back when trying on a jacket. Arch your back slightly to judge a fitted blouse. And stroll in shoes on a hard surface *and* carpet.

Don't give in

Ask yourself five key questions about the item you're trying on, recommends New York stylist Dayna Spitz: Do I love it? Do I feel great in it? Does it fit me well? Does it flatter me? Do I have at least two things to wear with it?

Know your price

When you find a miracle worker, like the work pants that make you look two inches taller, buy at full price. As for the sale rack: it's not a bargain if you won't wear it.

SPLURGE-WORTHY No-regrets, totally trendproof, absolutely-worth-the-extra-money buys

CLASSIC BAG
Never having to worry about whether you have something to carry with a suit or out to drinks? Priceless.

WOOL TROUSERS
Invest in a well-cut pair of high-quality menswear flannel, gabardine, wool or wool crêpe pants.

FINE WATCH
Instant, wear-every-where polish. Stick to classic styles like the Cartier tank; avoid ornate bezels.

KNEE BOOTS
Choose black or chocolate brown. The best last years, especially if you add rubber soles.

WOOL BLAZER
Look for a seasonless wool and a three- or four-button style to wear with everything from jeans to pencil skirts.

Quality Control

IN-STORE TRICKS FOR SUSSING OUT WHAT'S WORTH THE PRICE, WHAT'S NOT

Tips

SQUEEZE THE WOOL Scrunch the back of the wool coat you're considering and hold the fabric in your hand for a good 20 seconds. When you release, does your topper still look unrumpled and smooth, or is it wrinkled and bunched?

PARSE THE PATTERN Does that lovely floral print on a skirt or jacket line up perfectly across every seam? If not, leave it hanging.

LOOK FOR A LINING The best pieces are usually fully lined. If something is partially lined, look carefully at where the lining ends and make sure it doesn't show through to the front.

SIZE THE POCKETS You can probably live with 'em, but skimpy, shallow pockets are a sign that someone cut corners.

CHECK THE SEAMS Is there an allowance that will enable alterations if a jacket needs to be let out a bit or trousers need to be lengthened? Are the seams lying flat on the inside—not bulky, rumpled or uneven? Finally, since stitches per inch is another finishing standard, check that there isn't too much give when you pull apart the sides of the seam slightly from the inside.

$79

$300

WHY THE DIFFERENCE In one hand you hold a $79 cashmere sweater; in the other, one that sells for $300. They look the same, so why such a big difference? The No. 1 price factor is the fiber itself; the best cashmere sweaters are made with only the finest hairs handpicked from Mongolian goats once a year. (Look for "100 percent cashmere" on the label.) Cheaper sweaters start with slightly coarser hairs and are blended with other fibers. The upper end is also knit entirely by hand, as opposed to lockstitched. "Ply" isn't necessarily a cost concern; it denotes the thickness of the yarn. Bottom line: You'll generally have to spend at least $200 to get a pure cashmere sweater that will last—and look good—for years.

How to Save

BAGS If you're looking for a single handbag update for the season but are tired of the same old black and brown, consider neutral-friendly green, burgundy or orange.

PANTS Save on casual pants in fabrics like cotton blends or corduroy since you'll be throwing them in the wash, wearing them hard, and likely replacing them next season anyway.

COSTUME JEWELRY Cheaper, trendier chain stores you might never visit for clothing often have updated baubles and beads for less. Vintage stores also have great finds.

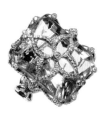

T-SHIRTS Tissue-soft Ts feel great but can get expensive thanks to all the treatments the cotton receives. If you find a stylish, if less heavenly, version for less, buy several in dark colors.

WORK CLOTHES Buy well-made basics like trousers and an A-line skirt in black and wear repeatedly. No one will notice if you recycle them regularly, especially if you mix up your tops and accessories.

LINGERIE Buy basic, everyday underwear and hosiery at outlets or discount chains such as Marshalls or Target. If you choose nude, seamless styles, you'll be able to get even more wear out of your basics.

For exclusive discounts every month, visit InStyle.com/dealsandsteals

Vintage Shopping

A QUICK GUIDE TO FINDING CHIC COLLECTIBLES

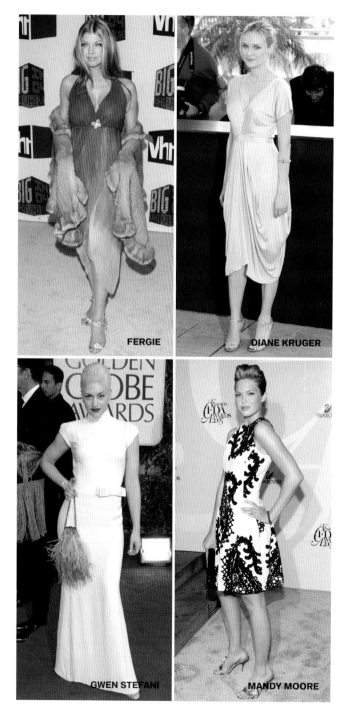

FERGIE

DIANE KRUGER

GWEN STEFANI

MANDY MOORE

WHAT'S IN A PRICE One hundred dollars for this disco dress, $10,000 for that one? Seemingly random prices come down to a few factors, says Cameron Silver, owner of L.A. vintage store Decades. They include: condition, wearability, provenance (straight from the original owner's wardrobe is best), and whether a piece is a hot collectible or by an important designer.

BREAKING IN "Accessories are a great way to start vintage shopping," Silver says. There are no pesky fit issues, you can look them over easily, and bargains are possible. Coats and little black dresses, she adds, are also great entry points, with designs that tend to be timeless.

POINT OF NO RETURN Forget having two weeks to make up your mind. "When you shop vintage, it's final sale," Silver says. Which means you really need to take your time to judge an item's condition. Examine it near a window, she advises, if a store doesn't have good lighting.

BARGAINING POWER Haggling is not unheard of, but there are tasteful ways to do it. Try a smile, and ask, "What's your friendliest price?"

THE RIGHT SIZE A 1950s size 8 is equivalent to about today's size 4. "Get past the number," Silver says, and try on what looks like it might work for you.

THAT SMELL If a musty odor is bothering you, you're probably better off passing. "A good store dry-cleans everything," Silver says, which means that what you smell is what you get .

THE FIND
Sixties patterned Pucci
bra and slip, $150, at
Decades Vintage
through Ebay

THE FIND
Fifties beaded wool
cardigan, $75, at thrift-
store Cobblestones,
New York City

THE FIND
Nineties Hermès
Birkin bag, $8,500, at
Loco boutique, East
Hampton, New York

THE FIND
Fifties Monet bracelet,
$75, and Napier ear-
rings, $125, at NYC flea
market Antiques Garage

SCORE! TIPS FOR SHOPPING AT FAVORITE VINTAGE SOURCES.
ONLINE Prices online are 40 to 50 percent less than at a high-end store, but since you can't examine items in person, make sure the site has a money-back guarantee. THRIFT STORES It can be hard to judge quality at a second-hand free-for-all, but a label that's woven and sewn down on all four sides indicates quality. FLEA MARKETS They're where the deals are on jumbo-size costume jewelry pieces from the forties that look cool now. VINTAGE BOUTIQUES Shop here for shoes and designer bags, but check interior linings and clasps on bags in particular.

Shopping Calendars

WHEN TO SHOP FOR WHAT, WITH TIPS FOR HOW TO BUY WISELY

JULY	OCTOBER	DECEMBER
fall arrivals	**markdowns begin**	**clearance sales**

JULY — fall arrivals

Good to know: Actually, "pre-fall" clothes arrive at better department stores as early as June, since most larger stores stagger their fall and spring deliveries over a couple of months. By late July you can successfully start shopping for your fall capsule wardrobe, those must-have building blocks that you can't compromise on in terms of color and cut. But new fall items arrive as late as September, and sometimes even October.

OCTOBER — markdowns begin

Get to know a store sales-woman well and she'll put you on her list of preferred customers, letting you know the exact day a sale will begin—or, if she really likes you, when the specific cashmere crew or beaded clutch you've been lusting after is first going to be reduced. Some department stores, like Lord & Taylor, will notify credit card holders of upcoming sales by mail and give them deeper incentives, by offering things like coupons.

DECEMBER — clearance sales

While many stores offer temporary doorbusters for Black Friday, the day after Thanksgiving, the deep discounts begin the week after Christmas. And big stores may be slashing earlier than ever before. Last year Saks Fifth Avenue made news by starting its clearance before the Christmas holiday. Coats, however, are not marked down until January and then disappear fast. Since they're such a key wardrobe building block, it's often not worth trying to hold out for this kind of basic.

FEBRUARY

spring arrivals

At better department stores, like Henri Bendel, resort wear arrives first in November and December, after its own runway previews. If you need something for an early winter trip and can't afford these higher-end designer threads, don't forget to try online resources (figleaves.com and cyberswim.com are two good picks with a variety of styles and sizes) or online and catalog retailers like J. Crew that offer their swimwear year-round.

APRIL

markdowns begin

While markdowns on summer dresses and capris start happening at department stores just after the merchandise arrives, swimsuits don't usually go on sale until after Memorial Day. Smaller boutiques tend to start markdowns on a less regimented basis— that is, whenever they see fit, depending on how business is going. Always ask about the return policy with any reduced or clearance item; rules tend to be stricter than with full-price items.

MEMORIAL DAY

clearance sales

Memorial Day signals the start of spring clearances. If you're buying clothes at the end of the season to hold until next spring, store them correctly in your closet, so white Ts don't dull and delicate camisoles don't get dusty. Keep in mind that summer items that seem fun and trendy now might not be as appealing next year. A good tip for controlling your clearance sale shopping habit? Divide by two the haul you'd like to bring to the checkout.

HOT BOUTIQUES

ATLANTA

BLUE GENES
Around 3400
Lenox Drive N.E.,
Suite 214
404-231-3400
Carries: Sacred Blue,
Habitual, Seven,
Valentino Roma,
Capital Tailors
Celebrity fans: Faith Hill,
Kanye West

AUSTIN

ALLENS BOOTS
1522 S. Congress Ave.
512-447-1413
Carries: Old Gringo,
Tony Lama, Lucchese

FACTORY PEOPLE
1325 S. Congress Ave.
512-440-8002
Carries: dozens of makers,
from Everett Parker
to Hysteric Glamour

FIVE OCEANS
1413 S. Congress Ave.
512-447-3483
Carries: Swimwear

**LUCY IN DISGUISE
WITH DIAMONDS**
1506 S. Congress Ave.
512-444-2002
Carries: costumes,
flapper dresses
Celebrity fan:
Gina Gershon

THERAPY
1113 S. Congress Ave.
512-326-2331
Carries: Mason by
Michelle Mason, Dessous,
Susana Monaco
Celebrity fan: Julia Roberts

BOSTON

ALPHA OMEGA JEWELERS
1380 Massachusetts Ave.
800-447-4367
Carries: Color Story,
A. Lange & Sohne
Celebrity fans: Ben Affleck, Sean
Combs, Teri Hatcher, Tim Robbins,
Kelly Rowland

LOUIS BOSTON
234 Berkeley St.
800-225-5135
Carries: clothing, accessories,

CHICAGO

FREESIA
3530 N. Southport Ave.
773-348-8670
Carries: shirts, accessories
Celebrity fan: Jessica Simpson

HEJFINA
1529 N. Milwaukee Ave.
773-772-0002
Carries: Earnest Sewn, Sonia
Rykiel, Isabel Marant, Edun
Celebrity fans: Orlando Bloom,
Maggie Gyllenhaal, Robin Tunney

ISABELLA FINE LINGERIE
1101 W. Webster Ave.
773-281-2352
Carries: Leigh Bantivoglio, Parah,
Le Mystère
Celebrity fans: Julia Roberts,
Jessica Simpson

JADE
1557 N. Milwaukee Ave.
773-342-5233
Carries: bohemian-style knits,
handbags, dresses and skirts by
designers like Candela NYC, lisli
Celebrity fans: Maggie Gyllenhaal,
Robin Tunney

JAKE
939 North Rush St.
312-664-5553
Carries: Be & D,
Botkier, Kooba,
Habitual, Cacharel
Celebrity fan: Kanye West

KRISTA K
3458 N. Southport Ave.
773-248-1967
Carries: Citizens of Humanity,
Marc by Marc Jacobs,
Catherine Malandrino,
Tibi, Theory,
Rebecca Taylor

P. 45
1643 N. Damen Ave.
773-862-4523
Carries: Flavio Olivera,
Toki Collection, Ya-Ya,
Eugenia Kim, Chip & Pepper
Celebrity fans: Laura Dern,
Maggie Gyllenhaal

RAIZY
1944 N. Damen Ave.
773-227-2221
Carries: lingerie from Tocca,
Le Mystère, Scott Barnes
Celebrity fan: Robin Tunney

RED HEAD BOUTIQUE
3450 N. Southport Ave.
773-325-9898
Carries: Cynthia Steffe,
Generra, Sanctuary,
Alice & Trixie, Amo & Bretti
Celebrity fan: Jessica Simpson

SHANE
3657 N. Southport Ave.
773-549-0179
Carries: Le Tigre, Three Dots,
Michael Star
Celebrity fan: Joan Cusack

SHOPGIRL
1206 W. Webster Ave.
773-935-7467
Carries: Trina Turk,
Juicy Couture,
Free People, Joe's Jeans
Celebrity fans: Liv Tyler,
Julia Roberts

TROUSSEAU
3543 N. Southport Ave.
773-472-2727
Carries: lingerie

LAS VEGAS

SCOOP
3500 Las Vegas Blvd.
702-734-0026
Carries: Theory, Jimmy Choo

TALULAH G
Boca Park Fashion Village
750 S. Rampart Blvd., Suite 13
702-932-7000
Carries: Stella McCartney,
Chloé, Anja Flint
Celebrity fans: Nikki Hilton,
Anna Kournikova

THE ATTIC
1018 S. Main St.
702-388-2848
Carries: vintage clothing
Celebrity fans: David Arquette,
Kelly Osbourne, David Spade

LOS ANGELES

APARTMENT 3
813 N. La Brea
323-939-3853
Carries: Cornichiwa,
Minnie Wilde,
Miko, Animall
Celebrity fans: Christina
Applegate, Hilary Duff,
Taryn Manning,
Alyssa Milano

BIRD
134 S. Robertson
310-205-6900
Carries: camisoles, flats
Celebrity fan: Cameron Diaz

CHAN LUU
112 S. Robertson
310-273-3527
Carries: in-store collection
Celebrity fans:
Mischa Barton,
Halle Berry

CURVE
154 N. Robertson
310-360-8008
Carries: C by Chloé,
Versus, Bella
Freud, Alice Roi

DARI
12184 Ventura Blvd.
818-762-3274
Carries: Sass & Bide,
Development, Jill Stuart,
Generra, Rebecca Taylor,
Sonia Rykiel
Celebrity fans: Rachel Bilson,
Hilary Duff, Teri Hatcher

DDC LAB
8906 Melrose Ave.
310-385-8085
Carries: in-house label
Celebrity fan: Joss Stone

DIAVOLINA
156 S. Robertson
310-550-1341
Carries: Costume National, Chloe,
Proenza Schouler, Grey Ant
Celebrity fan: Lindsay Lohan

ELYSE WALKER
15306 Antioch St., Pacific Palisades
310-230-8882
Carries: Stella McCartney,
Miu Miu, Prada
Celebrity fan: Jennifer Garner

ERICA COURTNEY
117 N. Robertson
310-858-6700
and 7465 Beverly Blvd.
323-938-2850
Carries: chandelier earrings,
cocktail rings, Tahitian pearls
Celebrity fan: Madonna

HARMONIE
2800 Abbot Kinney Blvd.,
Venice, Calif.
310-306-5059
Carries: Miguelina, Plenty by
Tracy Reese, Triple Five Soul
Celebrity fans: Faith Evans,
Julia Roberts

HILLARY RUSH
8222 W. Third St.
323-852-0088
Carries: L.A. Made, Twinkle,
Sunner, Nicholas K, Abaété
Celebrity fans: Mischa Barton,
Rachel Bilson

KITSON
115 S. Robertson
310-273-3527
Carries: True Religion,
Carlos Falchi
Celebrity fans: Jessica Simpson,
Gwen Stefani

LISA KLINE
136 S. Robertson
310-859-2652
Carries: Rebecca Taylor, Da-nang,
Tarina Tarantino, Vince
Celebrity fan: Jennifer Aniston

MA JOLIE
147 South Barrington Pl.
310-471-9545
Carries: Lotta, Blue Cult,
Ascension, David Galan
Celebrity fans: Mischa Barton, Eva
Longoria, Sharon Stone

MARC JACOBS
8409 Melrose
323-866-8255

MARNI
8460 Melrose Place
323-782-1101

SAMA
8460 Santa Monica Blvd.
323-654-6093
Carries: David Yurman,
Mikimoto, Marco Bicego
Celebrity fans: James
Gandolfini, Christina Ricci,
Jessica Simpson

SONYA OOTEN GEM BAR
238 N. Larchmont Blvd.
323-462-4453
Carries: Jewelry
Celebrity fans: Mariska Hargitay,
Nicole Kidman, Naomi Watts

STUDIO AT FRED SEGAL
500 Broadway, Santa Monica
310-394-8509
Carries: Fracas, Korres, Aesop
Celebrity fans: Jennifer Aniston,
Nicole Kidman, Michelle Pfeiffer

SUGAR ON LA BREA
633 N. La Brea, Suite A
323-965-0359

Carries: Chanel, Loom-state,
Sugar Babies, Nay-Nay
Celebrity fans: Kirsten Dunst,
Nicollette Sheridan

TED BAKER LONDON
131 N. Robertson
310-550-7855

THE WARDROBE DEPARTMENT
100 Universal City Plaza
800-864-8377
Carries: items celebs wore on
screen; designers include
Christian Lacroix, Carolina
Herrera, Valentino

THE WAY WE WORE
334 S. La Brea Ave.
323-937-0878
Carries: vintage clothes and
accessories
Celebrity fan: Kirsten Dunst

TORY BY TRB
142 S. Robertson
310-248-2612
Carries: bohemian caftans,
blouses and dresses
Celebrity fan:
Reese Witherspoon

TRACY FEITH
8446 Melrose
323-658-7464

MIAMI

AMERICAN APPAREL
720 Lincoln Rd.
305-672-1799
Carries: tanks, bikinis, baby Ts

BASE
939 Lincoln Rd.
305-531-6470
Carries: tanks,
army pants, jackets

Celebrity fans: Lauren
Hutton, Usher

CHROMA
920 Lincoln Rd.
305-695-8808
Carries: Mayle,
Sass & Bide, Lamb

DASZIGN
1663 Collins Ave.
305-531-5531
Carries: Lynne Larson, Catherine
Malandrino, Robert Rodriguez,
Lamb, James Perse, Heatherette
Celebrity fans: Jessica Alba,
Rachel Bilson, Eva Longoria

EN AVANCE
734 Lincoln Rd.
305-534-0337
Carries: Dsquared, Miguelina
Celebrity fans: Cameron Diaz,
Madonna

FLY BOUTIQUE
650 Lincoln Rd.
305-604-8508
Carries: vintage clothing
Celebrity fans: Cameron Diaz,
Lenny Kravitz, Kate Moss

JULIAN CHANG
1665 Michigan Ave.
305-538-2242
Carries: store-label dresses,
tops, pants
Celebrity fans: Angelina Jolie,
Gabrielle Union

LEO
640 Collins Ave.
305-531-6550
Carries: Heatherette,
Cacharel, Imitation of Christ,
Samantha Treacy
Celebrity fans: Kelis, Nas

MARTIER
103 Lincoln Rd.
305-604-1877
Carries: Antik Denim,
Ginger & Java

ROSA CHA
830 Lincoln Rd.
305-538-7883
Carries: swimsuits
Celebrity fan: Britney Spears

SASPARILLA
1630 Pennsylvania Ave.
305-532-6611
Carries: Gucci, Dolce & Gabbana,
Romeo Gigli

STEAM ON SUNSET
5828 Sunset Drive
305-669-9991
Carries: Matthew Williamson
Celebrity fans: Jada Pinkett Smith,
Catherine Zeta-Jones

NEW YORK CITY

AVIANNE & CO.
28 W. 47th St.
212-398-0611
Carries: custom-made diamond
pieces
Celebrity fans: 50 Cent, Jimmy
Fallon, Jamie Foxx, Jada Pinkett
Smith

CALYPSO
815 Madison Ave.
212-585-0310
Carries: high-end
bohemian clothing
Celebrity fan: Nicollette Sheridan

CYNTHIA ROWLEY
376 Bleecker St.
212-242-3803
Carries: embroidered dresses
and colorful shoes

Celebrity fans: Maggie Gyllenhaal,
Hilary Swank

DARLING
1 Horatio St.
646-336-6966
Carries: Cynthia Steffe, Earth
Speaks, Jill Michelle, plus vintage
Celebrity fans: Sarah Jessica
Parker, Keri Russell

DERNIER CRI
869 Washington St.
212-242-6061
Carries: Vivienne Westwood,
Mara Hoffman, Katharine Sise
Celebrity fans: Lindsay Lohan,
Julianne Moore, Liv Tyler

ELIZABETH CHARLES
639 1/2 Hudson St.
212-243-3201
Carries: Lover, Zambesi
Celebrity fans: Sandra Bullock,
Hilary Swank, Uma Thurman

ERICA TANOV
204 Elizabeth St.
212-334-8020
Carries: dresses

EUGENIA KIM
203 E. Fourth St.
212-673-9787
Carries: hats, fedoras
Celebrity fans: Jennifer Lopez,
Gwyneth Paltrow

INTERMIX
365 Bleecker St.
212-929-7180
Carries: Stella McCartney, Lolli,
lisli, Costume National, Chloe,
Diane von Furstenberg, Vince

JAMIN PUECH
247 Elizabeth St.
212-431-5200
Carries: ornate bags

Celebrity fans: Claire Danes,
Sarah Jessica Parker,
Natalie Portman

KEY
41 Grand St.
212-334-5707
Carries: vintage shoes,
belts and jewelry
Celebrity fans: Lauren Graham,
Brooke Shields

LULU GUINNESS
394 Bleecker St.
212-367-2120
Carries: handbags and accessories
Celebrity fans: Marisa Tomei

MARC JACOBS ACCESSORIES
385 Bleecker St.
212-924-6126

NOM DE GUERRE
640 Broadway
212-253-2891
Carries: Nike, Absurd, Noah,
Rogan, Asfour, Red Label
Celebrity fans: Paul Bettany,
Jennifer Connelly, Mos Def,
Jude Law, Sienna Miller

OLIVE & BETTE'S
384 Bleecker St.
212-206-0036
Carries: Cynthia Steffe, Paige,
James, Tamara Henriques,
Wendy Mink
Celebrity fans: Sarah Jessica
Parker, Julia Roberts

PLUM
124 Ludlow St.
212-529-1030
Carries: Nicholas K, Lizzie
Fortunato
Celebrity fans: Shannon Elizabeth,
Macy Gray, Adrian Grenier

SATYA JEWELRY
330 Bleecker St.
212-243-7313
Carries: yoga-inspired jewelry, malas
Celebrity fan: Susan Sarandon

SEVEN NEW YORK
110 Mercer St.
646-654-0156
Carries: Proenza Schouler, Preen, Sweetface
Celebrity fans: Mary J. Blige, Lindsay Lohan, Madonna, Chloë Sevigny

SHOWROOM 64
106 Greenwich Ave.
800-646-7864
Carries: gifts, T-shirts, hats, jewelry
Celebrity fans: Minnie Driver, Julianne Moore, Liv Tyler

VERVE
336 Bleecker St.
212-675-6693
Carries: Chie Mihara, Kalliste, Kooba, Rafe

PHILADELPHIA

CHIC BELLA
2100 Chestnut St.
215-972-0707
Carries: Grass Jeans, Hudson, BCBG
Celebrity fans: Eve, Jada Pinkett Smith

LEEHE FAI
133 S. 18th St.
215-564-6111
Carries: Anna Sui, Tracy Reese, Trina Turk and Velvet
Celebrity fans: Cameron Diaz, Jessica Simpson, Liv Tyler

SAN FRANCISCO

ALLA PRIMA
539 Hayes St.
415-864-8180
Carries: La Perla, Cosabella, Only Hearts

AZALEA
411 Hayes St.
415-861-9888
Carries: Sonia/Sonia Rykiel

BACKSPACE
508 Hayes St.
415-701-7112
Carries: 7 for All Mankind, Grey Ant, Sass & Bide
Celebrity fans: Courteney Cox

BULO
418 Hayes St.
415-255-4939
Carries: shoes, bags, sunglasses

DISH
541 Hayes St.
415-252-5997
Carries: Yanuk, Viv & Ingrid, Meli Melo, Citizens of Humanity
Celebrity fan: Sheryl Crow

DYLAN
1506 Vallejo St.
415-931-8721
Carries: Kaviar and Kind Jewelry, Paige Premium Denim, Chloé, Earnest Sewn, True Religion, Vince
Celebrity fan: Nicole Richie

GIMME SHOES
416 Hayes St.
415-864-0691
Carries: Miu Miu, Prada, Robert Clergerie, Sigerson Morrison

NIDA
544 and 564 Hayes St.
415-552-4670
and 2163 Union St.
415-928-4670
Carries: Paul & Joe, Costume National, Helmut Lang, Pucci, Avant Toi
Celebrity fans: Nicole Richie, Mena Suvari

SEATTLE

PED
1115 First Ave.
206-292-1767
Carries: Audley, Cydwoq, Orla Kiely, Calleen Cordero
Celebrity fans: Jennifer Aniston, Alanis Morissette

ZOVO LINGERIE
4612 26th Ave.
206-525-9686
Carries: Simone Perele, Le Mystère, Princess Tam Tam, Kai
Celebrity fans: Patrick Dempsey, Kate Hudson, Sarah McLachlan

WASHINGTON, D.C.

SUGAR
1633 Wisconsin Ave. N.W.
202-333-5331
Carries: Tibi, Viv & Ingrid, Lauren Moffatt
Celebrity fans: Barbara and Jenna Bush, Gabrielle Union

SOME FUN WEB SITES

GENERAL CLOTHING

activeendeavors.com

adampluseve.com

ae.com

aloharag.com

americanapparel.net

anntaylor.com

anthropologie.com

ardenb.com

armaniexchange.com

babymabels.com

bally.com

bananarepublic.com

bebe.com

blaec.com

bluebeeonline.com

bluefly.com

bodenusa.com

chipandpepper.com

designsbystephene.com

dkny.com

edressme.com

eluxury.com

expressfashion.com

forever21.com

fornarina.com

fredflare.com

girlshop.com

guess.com

intermixonline.com

jacquelinejarrot.com

jcrew.com

kaneesha.com

kipepeo74.com

labellosangeles.com

lovetanjane.com

mavi.com

millabymail.com

neimanmarcus.com

net-a-porter.com

newportnews.com

nordstrom.com

oliveandbettes.com

pinkmascara.com

polkadotsandmoonbeams.com

polo.com

ravinstyle.com

revolveclothing.com

rocawear.com

ronherman.com

saks.com

searlenyc.com

shop603.com

shopbop.com

shopkitson.com

shoptwigs.com

talbots.com

urbanoutfitters.com

vivre.com

vondutch.com

yoox.com

BAGS, SHOES AND ACCESSORIES

coach.com

cottonpalace.com

ellevenup.com

nicnorman.com

skechers.com

sportiela.com

tiviwear.com

tresjolie.com

zappos.com

JEWELRY

fragments.com

globalgirlfriend.com

kaviarjewelry.com

mayyeung.com

tiffany.com

whitetrashcharms.com

LINGERIE

agentprovocateur.com

allthingsbeneath.com

balicompany.com

barenecessities.com

barelythere.com

bedheadpjs.com

brasmyth.com

donnaloren.com

figleaves.com

flexees.com

gapbody.com

laperla.com

myla.com

thelittleflirt.com

victoriassecret.com

SWIMWEAR

aerinrose.com

belabumbum.com

cyberswim.com

everythingbutwater.com

figleaves.com

maliamills.com

vixswimwear.com

credits →

CLOTHING AND ACCESSORIES, PHOTOGRAPHY

CLOTHING AND ACCESSORY CREDITS

P. 5 Kate's Paperie

P. 43 plastic shoe drawers: Container Store; shoe boxes: Closet Fetish; shoe organizer: Hold Everything; bookends: Pylones Soho

P. 46 skirt: Elie Tahari, shirt: Stella Forest, shoe: Stuart Weitzman

P. 49 top to bottom, left to right: French Connection, Luciano Barbera, David Meister, Alvin Valley, Diane von Furstenberg, Paige Premium Denim, Paul & Joe, Charles Tyrwhitt, Loro Piana, Isaac Mizrahi for Target, Moschino, S. Edelman, Coach, Manolo Blahnik

P. 50 clockwise, from top left: Club Monaco, Laundry, A.P.C., French Connection

P. 51 top to bottom: Anthropologie, H&M

P. 52 top to bottom: Sportmax, Lands' End, Edward An

P. 53 top to bottom: Talbot's, Refrigiwear, Ralph Lauren Blue Label

P. 54 left to right: Ann Taylor, Theory

P. 55 Tocca

P. 56-57 look 1, suit: Theory, top: Adam & Eve; look 2, suit: Theory, top: Votrenom; look 3, skirt: Theory, top: Anne Taylor, vest: J.Crew; look 4, jacket: Theory, top:

Magaschoni, jeans: Joe's Jeans, bag: Laura Rosnovsky

P. 58 clockwise, from top left: Normandy Monroe, DVF, Ralph Lauren Black Label, Ports 1961

P. 59 top to bottom: Maxstudio.com, Dolce & Gabbana

P. 60 clockwise, from top left: Charles Tyrwhitt, Thomas Pink, DKNY, Three Dots

P. 61 top to bottom: Milly, Rozae Nichols

P. 62-63 blouse: Blugirl by Blumarine; look 1, sweater and brooch: Ascension, jeans: Blue Cult, Bag: Philosophy di Alberta Ferretti, Pumps: Delman; look 2, sweater: Elie Tahari, skirt: Yigal Azrouël, necklace: R.J. Graziano, Clutch: Susan Fitch, Sandals: 12th Street by Cynthia Vincent, Sophea Parros; look 3, jacket: Banana Republic, belt: Liz Claiborne, skirt: Boden, flats: Banana Republic; look 4, sweater: Ginger, pants: Joe's Jeans, bag: Adrienne Vittadini, wedges: Stuart Weitzman

P. 64 clockwise, from top left: Theory, Max & Co., Agnès B., Stella McCartney

P. 65 top to bottom: Express, BCBG

P. 66 Dolce & Gabbana

P. 67 Emporio Armani

P. 68 clockwise, from top left: spanx.com, Loro Piana, BCBG, Paul & Joe

P. 69 top to bottom: Donna Karan Collection, Rick Owens

P. 70-71 sweater: Vince; look 1, shirt: David Meister, pants: Raven, belt: Sun Ray, shoes: Juicy Couture, bag: Taryn Rose; look 2, camisole: Rebecca Taylor, shorts: La Rok, shoes: Fendi; look 3, top: Adam & Eve, jeans: Sass & Bide, boots: Max Mara, bag: Tory Burch; look 4, camisole: Adam & Eve, skirt: Robert Rodriguez, shoes: Olivia Morris

P. 72 clockwise from top left: Luciano Barbera, Ungaro Fuchsia, Calvin Klein, H&M

P. 73 top to bottom: Daslu, Milly

P. 74-75 jacket: Fornarina; look 1, tank: Theory, jeans: Paige Premium Denim; look 2, shirt: Anna Paul, belt: Vince, pants: Raven; look 3, shirt: Casch, skirt: BCBG, clutch: Max Mara

P. 76 clockwise, from top left: MéliMélo, Habitual, Joe's Jeans, 7 for All Mankind

P. 77 top to bottom: Saltworks, Levi's Premium

P. 78-79 jeans: Miss Sixty; look 1, top: Tufi Duek, necklace: Marnie Rocks, flats: Jimmy Choo; look 2, sweater: Vince, tank: Gap, necklace: Exex Jewelry, boots: Bally; look 3, top: Shoshanna, pumps: Giuseppe Zanotti Design; look 4, jacket: Tory by TRB, blouse: Juicy Couture, bag: Francesco Biasia, slingbacks: Stuart Weitzman

P. 80 clockwise, from top left: Bottega Veneta, Furla, Bulga, Donald J Pliner

P. 81 top to bottom: Alberta Ferretti, Sergio Rossi

P. 82 clockwise, from top left: Bettye Muller, LD Tuttle, Cynthia Rowley, Manolo Blahnik

P. 83 clockwise, from top left: Jean-Michel Cazabat, Lambertson Truex, Sigerson Morrison, Calvin Klein

P. 84 work look 1, watch: Links of London, suit: Kenneth Cole New York, cardigan: Elie Tahari, bag: Kate Spade, shoes: Rafe, shirt: Liz Claiborne; work look 2, pants: Mint, vest: Whim, shoes: S. Edelman, bag: Michael Graves, watch: Pedre, earrings: Giselle, pin: New York & Co., shirt with tie: Parameter

P. 85 work look 3, earrings: Crislu, sweater: White + Warren, shirt: Agnès B., belt: Suzi Roher, purse: Moschino Cheap and Chic, glasses: Horchow, shoes: Enzo Angiolini, skirt: Kay Unger; work Look 4, shirt: Allen B. by Allen Schwartz; skirt: Gap; belt: DKNY, purse: Jana Feifer, earrings: Gabrielle Sanchez, bracelet: Sandra Goodkind, shoes: Moschino

P. 86 work look 5, jacket: Teenflo, blouse: Milly, shirt: Chico's, earrings: St. John, tie belt: Charles Tyrwhitt, purse: DKNY, watch: Swiss Army, shoes: St. John, jeans: Capital Tailors; work look 6, earrings: Deanna Hamro, jacket: Kulson, cardigan: Plenty by Tracy Reese, shirt: Burning Torch,

gloves: Ann Taylor, skirt: Supply and Demand, purse: Lulu Guinness, shoes: Miss Sixty

P. 87 work look 7, sweater: Express, shirt: Alâra, necklace: Roxanne Assoulin for Lee Angel, belt: Coz, purse: Gap, PDA case: LAI, shoes: Sergio Rossi, pants: Nanette Lepore; work look 8, blazer: Lisli, pants: Anne Klein New York, shoes: Vera Wang, purse: Gap, brooch: Erickson Beamon, earrings: Blonka for Che1020, shirt: Andrea Jovine

P. 88 weekend look 1, jacket: United Colors of Benetton, skirt: Alice Roi, vest: Levi's, sweater: Sisley, purse: Ralph Lauren, bracelet: Versani, boots: United Colors of Benetton, earrings: Stacy Westcarr; weekend look 2, sweater: Ralph Lauren Blue Label, belt: Stitch's, pocket watch: Eddie Bauer, jeans: Streets Ahead, shirt: Company Ellen Tracy, earrings: Gas Bijoux, purse: Dooney & Bourke, boots: Max & Co.

P. 89 weekend look 3, sweater: H&M, shirt: Gap, watch: Tommy Bahama, pants: Sisley, sneakers: Converse, tote: Express; weekend look 4, earrings: 1928 Jewelry, sweater: Lauren by Ralph Lauren, shirt: Alidio Michelli, jacket: Unconditional State, glasses: Kenneth Cole New York, belt: René Lezard, pants: Boss Black, watch: Patricia Urquiola, purse: Kenzo, sneakers: Tretorn

P. 90 weekend look 5, jacket: Armani Jeans, jeans: Rock & Republic, shirt: Hale-Bob, purse: Bulga, shoes: Cynthia Rowley, earrings: Avenue; weekend look 6,

cardigan: the Wrights, jacket: J. Crew, necklace: Malin, purse: Tocca, scarf: Lisli, shirt: Lauren by Ralph Lauren, pants: MéliMélo, watch: Marchand de Legumes, shoes: Sigerson Morrison, earrings: JC Penney

P. 91 weekend look 7, jacket: Schumacher, vest: Isaac Mizrahi for Target, shirt: A. Cheng, watch: Hermès, earrings: New York & Company, gloves: Dooney & Bourke, purse: Moschino, boots: Børn, pants: Isaac Mizrahi for Target; weekend look 8, jacket: Free Country, sunglasses: Selima Optique, earrings: Gas Bijoux, shirt: Splendid, pants: Postcard, purse: Chanel, watch: Timex, ice skates: L.L. Bean

P. 93 top to bottom, left to right: David Rodriguez, Lela Rose, Calvin Klein Collection, Siena Studio, Agnès B., Lauren by Ralph Lauren, Banana Republic, Rachel Reinhardt, Verve, BCBG Max Azria, Manolo Blahnik, Eugenia Kim

P. 94-95 dress: David Rodriguez; look 1, jacket: Shoshanna, necklace: Isaac Manevitz for Ben-Amun, clutch: BCBG Max Azria, pumps: Giorgio Armani; look 2, shrug: Cassin, cuffs: Kenneth Jay Lane, heels: Alexandra Neel; look 3, belt: Lai, clutch: Lauren Merkin, shoes: Christian Louboutin

P. 96 clockwise, from top left: Dolce & Gabbana, Rodo, Escada, Donald J Pliner

P. 97 top to bottom: Clara Kasavina, Judith Leiber

P. 98 clockwise, from top left: Eugenia Kim, Kenneth Jay Lane for Hollywould, Aldo, Sergio Rossi

P. 99 clockwise, from top left: Dior by John Galliano, Nine West, Christian Lacroix, Oscar de la Renta

P. 100 evening look 1, jacket: The Limited, shirt: Schumacher, bolero: Bernardo, earrings: Robindira Unsworth, purse: Adrienne Vittadini, shoes: Moschino Cheap and Chic, pants: Raven; evening look 2, dress: maxstudio.com, purse: Ponchette by Melanie Dizon, earrings: Roxanne Assoulin for Lee Angel, bracelet: Gabrielle Sanchez, shoes: Sergio Rossi, dress: Jennifer Nicholson

P. 101 evening look 3, necklace: Viktoria Hayman, earrings: Ross-Simons, bracelets: Lazuz Collection, bag: Rodo, shoes: Juan Antonio Lopez; evening look 4, shirt: M.H. Maglia, camisole: Felina, earrings: R.J. Graziano, bracelet: Lara Bohinc 107, pants: H Hilfiger, shoes: Jill Stuart, purse: Isabella Fiore

P. 102 evening look 5, pants: Ingwa, shirt: Nikka, earrings: Beaux Bijoux, bag: Elisa Atheniense, shoes: Sergio Rossi; evening look 6, jacket: Bernardo, skirt: Helen Wang, purse: Lauren Scherr, shirt: Valentino Red, belt: Suzi Roher, earrings: Roxanne Assoulin for Lee Angel, bracelet: Lenore Solmo, shoes: Nina Shoes

P. 103 evening look 7, dress: Boaz, necklace, earrings, and bracelet: Forever 21, purse: Banana

Republic, shoes: Banana Republic; evening look 8, camisole: Lia Kes, belt: Jill Stuart, pants: Frankie B., purse: Elaine Turner, shoes: Beverly Feldman

P. 104 bag: Kate Spade, shoes: J.Crew, skirt: Nanette Lepore

P. 107 top to bottom, left to right: James Perse, Mary Green, Gap, Kors Michael Kors, Beth Bowley, Sue Wong, Milly, Ralph by Ralph Lauren, Coach, Maxx New York, Lambertson Truex, Enzo Angiolini, Lisa Curran, Matta

P. 108 clockwise, from top left: Ralph Lauren, Marc Jacobs, Burberry, Deborah Hampton

P. 109 top to bottom: Ann Taylor, Banana Republic

P. 110 clockwise, from top left: Milly, Ann Taylor Loft, Paper Denim & Cloth, Max Mara

P. 111 top to bottom: Dressbarn, Izod

P. 112 sweater: J.Crew; look 1, Dress: Tibi, Necklace: Viktoria Hayman; look 2, top: Diane von Furstenberg, pants: Express, bag: Malini Murjani

P. 113 jacket: Theory; look 1, bag: Kate Spade, pants: Raven; look 2, dress: Catherine Malandrino, clutch: Jalda

P. 114 clockwise, from top left: James Perse, Ron Herman, Intermix, Anthropologie

P. 115 top to bottom: Mary Green, Cynthia Vincent

P. 116-117 shirt: Charles Tyrwhitt; look 1, skirt: DKNY, bracelet: Givenchy, sandals: House of Deréon; look 2, sweater: Lauren Active by Ralph Lauren, skirt: PF Flyers, shoes: Diesel Footwear; look 3, necklace: Kendra Scott Design, jeans: Anio, belt: Frank & Kahn, flats: Anne Klein New York; look 4, jacket and trousers: CK Calvin Klein, pumps: Manolo Blahnik

P. 118 clockwise, from top left: Vince, Splendid, Velvet by Graham & Spencer, C&C California

P. 119 top to bottom: American Apparel, James Perse

P. 120 clockwise, from top left: Temperley, BCBGirls, Lacoste, Sue Wong

P. 121 top to bottom: Catherine Malandrino, Stephanie Schaich

P. 122 clockwise from top left: Beth Bowley, Eddie Bauer, Chaiken, Plenty by Tracy Reese

P. 123 top to bottom: Sharagano, Michael Kors

P. 124 dress: Nanette Lepore; look 1, shirt: 7 for All Mankind; look 2, jacket: Adam & Eve

P. 125 skirt: Nanette Lepore; look 1, tank: Tse Say, bag: Moyna; look 2, top: Nanette Lepore, sweater: J.Crew

P. 126 clockwise, from top left: Forever 21, Vince, DKNY Jeans, Trovata

P. 127 top to bottom: Gap, BCBGirls

P. 128-129 shorts: Denim, CYN; look 1, t-shirt: Alberta Ferretti, watch: Michael Michael Kors, bag: Banana Republic, wedges: DKNY; look 2, top: Tracy Reese, clutch: Lauren Merkin, bangles: Sheila Fajl, sandals: Constança Basto; look 3, jacket: BCBGirls, t-shirt: Forever 21, bag: Rebecca Minkoff, wedges: Kate Spade

P. 130 Ralph Lauren Collection

P. 132 clockwise from top left: Nautica, Nautica, Sportmax, Victoria's Secret

P. 133 top to bottom: Be Creative, OMO Norma Kamali, Lisa Curran Swim, Eres

P. 134 left to right: Lisa Curran, Tommy Bahama

P. 135 left to right: Juicy Couture, La Blanca

P. 136 clockwise, from top left: Coach, Maxx New York, Luella Bartley, Kate Spade

P. 137 top to bottom: Coach, Andrea Stuart

P. 138 clockwise, from top left: Seychelles, H Hilfiger, Rafe, Steve Madden

P. 139 clockwise, from top left: Gap, Cesare Paciotti, Enzo Angiolini, Casadei

P. 140 work look 1, earrings: Patch NYC, bracelets: Pono, shirt: Sportmax, cardigan: Nanette Lepore, skirt: Sportmax, shoes: Enzo Angiolini, bag: Anya Hindmarch; work look 2, earrings: Dara at Fragments, clutch: Abas, cuff: Hermès, pants: Kingslee Greene, jacket: Biya, shirt: Jessie Della Femina, shoes: Constança Basto

P. 141 work look 3, earrings: Jenny Sheriff, watch: Pedre, brooch: Roxanne Assoulin for Lee Angel, sweater: J.Crew, shirt: Lauren by Ralph Lauren, skirt: To the Max, bag: New York & Co., shoes: H Hilfiger; work look 4, earrings: Emporio Armani, bracelets: Kiln Enamel, bag: Putu by J. MacLear, shirt: Pink Tartan, skirt: Pink Tartan, shoes: Jimmy Choo, sunglasses: Selima Optique

P. 142 work look 5, necklace: Anthropologie, pants: Banana Republic, shirt: APC, belt: Leatherock, bracelet: Bellissima, bag: Anthropologie, shoes: Frederick's of Hollywood; work look 6, earrings: Mimi Golzer, shirt: Company Ellen Tracy, skirt: Perry Ellis Women's, belt: Valentino, purse: Valentino, watch: Emporio Armani, shoes: Lambertson Truex

P. 143 work look 7, earrings: Agatha, shirt: Charles Tyrwhitt, tie: Charles Tyrwhitt, purse: Marc Jacobs, shoes: Heroes for Cesare Paciotti; work look 8, earrings: Paul Morelli, shirt: Ralph Lauren Black Label, sweater: Lands' End, brooch: Givenchy, jeans: Joe's Jeans, bag: Jana Feifer, shoes: Daniblack

P. 144 weekend look 1, earrings: New York & Co., tunic: Alpana Bawa, jeans: Grass Jeans, watch: Timex X-Factor by Matthew Williamson, bag: Longchamp, shoes: Matthew Williamson, tank with crystal trim: Pamela Jo; weekend look 2, tank: Michael Stars, skirt: Hartnell, bracelets: Aid Through Trade, tote: Free People, shoes: Havaianas

P. 145 weekend look 3, shirt: Necessary Objects, shorts: Dickies Girl, flower pin: Perry Ellis Women's, bag: Old Navy, shoes: Softsports; weekend look 4, earrings: Soixante Neuf, shirt with floral pin: Realities, belt: Dockers, jeans: Dickies Girl, bracelets: Spiegel, bag: Old Navy, shoes: Old Navy

P. 146 weekend look 5, earrings: Kenneth Cole New York, bracelets: Nine West, bolero: The Limited, tank: Reba, belt: Old Navy, shorts: Bebe, bag: Victoria's Secret Catalogue, shoes: J. Jill; weekend look 6, earrings: Saya Hibino, shirt: Orla Kiely, skirt: In the Now, necklace: Urban Outfitters, watch: BCBG Max Azria, bag: Worthington, shoes: Kate Spade

P. 147 weekend look 7, jacket: Nuala by Puma, cotton wrap: Megan Park, earrings: Jill Schwartz, camisole: Riley, pants: Ella Moss, shoes: Tatami by Birkenstock, earrings: Target; weekend look 8, dress: Muchacha, shirt: Beautiful People, necklace: Arena CPH for Fashioncamp, bag: Elissa Bloom, shoes: BCBG Max Azria

P. 148 evening look 1, dress: Jill Stuart, earrings: Erika Pena, clutch: Kathrine Baumann, shoes: Hollywould, earrings: Romy Ivsic; evening look 2, shirt: ECI, pants: Ascension, bracelet: Gerard Yosca, bag: Jana Feifer, shoes: Moschino

P. 149 evening look 3, jacket: Sisley, earrings: JC Penney, clutch: BCBG Max Azria, shoes: BCBGirls, bracelet: Elements/Jill Schwartz, pants: Spiegel; evening look 4, earrings: Beaux Bijoux, dress: Shoshanna, watch: Guess Watches, bag: Banana Republic, shoes: Colin Stuart for Victoria's Secret

P. 150 evening look 5, earrings: ice.com, sweater: Hidy Ng, dress: Tracy Reese, bracelets: the Pearl Outlet, bag: Franchi, shoes: Beverly Feldman; evening look 6, scarf: Newport News, earrings: Forever21.com, bracelets: Pade Vavra, cardigan: Bebe, tank: ABS by Allen Schwartz, pants: Lauren by Ralph Lauren, bag: Lauren Merkin, shoes: Spiegel

P. 151 evening look 7, dress: Reyes, bangles: Arden B., clutch: Tivi, shoes: Philosophy di Alberta Ferretti; evening look 8, earrings: Nancy Dobbs Owen, jacket: Gap, shirt: Express Design Studio, pants: Victoria's Secret Catalogue; evening look 8, watch: Hotkiss, bag: Elliott Lucca, shoes: Carlos by Carlos Santana

P. 154: Gap Body

P. 156 clockwise, from top left: Bali, Wacoal, Lilyette, Le Mystère

P. 157 clockwise, from top left: Fashion Forms, Gap Body, Champion, Maidenform

P. 158 clockwise, from top left: Lilo, Curvation, Body Wrap by Christina America, Inc., TC Fine Shapewear

P. 159 clockwise, from top left: American Eagle Outfitters, Maidenform, Flexees, Donna Karan New York

P. 162 clockwise, from top left: Kwiat, Orly Baruch, Fortunoff

P. 163 top to bottom, Emporio Armani, Hamilton

P. 164 clockwise, from top left: Erica Courtney, Annette Ferdinandsen, Arika C. Jewelry, Ileana Makri

P. 165 Donna Distefano

166 left: Diane von Furstenberg; right: Lacoste

P. 168 long coat: Jones New York Collection, blouse: Jones New York Signature, pants: City DKNY, tote: Talene Reilly, cardigan: J.Crew, dress: Graham & Spencer, wedge: Dooney & Bourke, bag: Seychelles, camisole: Gap

P. 170 jacket: Calvin Klein, jeans: Joe's Jeans, sunglasses: Christian Roth, blouse: Votre Nom, skirt: Fei by Anthropologie, shoes: Taryn Rose, shorts: DKNY

P. 172 shirt: Lands' End, bikini: Eberjey, hat: Lacoste, dress: Trina Turk, bag: Redfish Design, shoe: Rafe

P. 174 blazer and pants: Theory, scarf: Echo, dress: David Meister, coat: Express Design Studio, sweater: Lands' End, shirt: Ann Taylor, shoes: Banana Republic

P. 176 shoe: Tory Burch, wallet: Lambertson Truex, keychain: Coach

P. 179 left to right: Louis Vuitton, Express Design Studio, Cartier, Andrew Stevens, Luciano Barbera

P. 180 top to bottom: Michael Kors, Loro Piana

P. 181 clockwise, from top left: Banana Republic, Express Design Studio, Craig Taylor, Juicy Couture

MICHAEL GERMANA/
UPI/LANDOV
p. 18, Queen Latifah, right

GETTY
p. 182, Mandy Moore

JANET GOUGH/CELEBRITY
p. 22, Michelle Williams

SABRINA GRANDE
p. 49, work dress, v-neck sweater,
everyday purse, flat; p. 52, cashmere, shearling; p. 53; p. 68,
v-neck sweater; p. 69, oversize;
p. 80, drawstring; p. 100-103;
p. 107, cotton cardigan, thong
sandals, open-toe work shoes;
p. 110, cardigan; p. 114, cap-sleeve;
p. 121, empire, shirt; p. 140-151;
p. 168, long coat and structured
tote, structured purse, wedge,
camisole, jersey dress; p. 170;
p. 172, swimsuit and cover-up, hat;
p. 174; p. 180, black sweater, white
sweater; p. 181, purse

STEVE GRANITZ/WIREIMAGE
p. 109, Lucy Lui

AMY GRAVES/WIREIMAGE
p. 23, Faith Hill

JENNIFER GRAYLOCK/JPI
p. 33, Sienna Miller, left

FRAZER HARRISON/GETTY
p. 95, Natalie Portman

NICK HARVEY/WIREIMAGE
p. 26, Gwyneth Paltrow

DAN HERRICK/KPA/ZUMA
p. 25, Kate Bosworth

DAN HERRICK/ZUMA
p. 69, Hilary Swank

GABRIELLA
IMPERATORI-PENN
p. 162, diamond studs, pearls

INFGOFF
p. 25, Eve

DEVON JARVIS
p. 49, jacket; p. 58, flare; p. 64,
boot-cut pants; p. 72, basic blazer;
p. 114, tank; p. 126, drawstring; p.
179, wool blazer; p. 181, black tee

NORMAN JEAN ROY
p. 6

JILL JOHNSON/JPI
p. 111, Joy Bryant

JONATHAN KANTOR
p. 83, flat boot

ROGER KARNBAD
p. 123, Kristin Davis

JON KOPALOFF/FILMMAGIC
p. 77, Molly Sims

PASCAL JUYOT/AFP/GETTY
p. 19, Cameron Diaz, left

DIMITRIOS KAMBOURIS/
WIREIMAGE
p. 21, Rachel McAdams; p. 55, Kate
Winslet; p. 115, Rebecca Romijn

HENRY LAMB/
PHOTOWIRE/BEIMAGES
p. 165, Sarah Jessica Parker

DAVID LAWRENCE
p. 10; p. 46; p. 49, jeans, black

pumps; p. 58, pleated, full; p. 64,
tweed; p. 65, cropped; p. 82,
classic pump; p. 104; p. 108, double-breasted; p. 109, dressy; p. 111,
embellished; p. 120, halter; p. 126,
short shorts, p. 139, thongs; p. 168,
cardigan; p. 176; p. 179, classic
bag, wool trousers; p. 181, pants

JOHN LAWTON
p. 107, sarong; p. 137, beach tote

PASCAL LE SEGRETAIN/
GETTY
p. 61, Katie Holmes

SVEND LINDBAEK
p. 72, velvet; p. 82, loafer pump,
pointed-toe flat, kitten heel; p. 83,
tall boot; ballerina flat, ankle boot;
p. 93, evening pump; p. 98, satin,
black, metallic strappy; p. 99,
ankle-strap, velvet, peep-toe
pump, slingback

LAWRENCE LUCIER/
FILMMAGIC
p. 15, Kate Hudson, left

MARK MAINZ/GETTY
p. 23, Kate Beckinsale

CARLEY MARGOLIS/
FILMMAGIC
p. 21, Sarah Jessica Parker;
p. 127, Eve

KURT MARKUS
p. 93, skirt, satin camisole

CHARLES MASTERS
p. 107, cotton shorts, trench;
p. 108, trench, color; p. 120,
fluttery

CHAYO MATA
p. 49, white shirt; p. 60, white; p. 62-63; p. 66-67; p. 76, trouser, high-back, boot-cut, skinny, cropped, relaxed; p. 78-79; p. 93, little black dress; p. 94; p. 85, simply sexy little black dress on model; p. 116-117; p. 156-159

JEFFREY MAYER/ WIREIMAGE
p. 28, Sigourney Weaver

HENRY MCGEE/GLOBE
p. 29, Jane Fonda

FRANCESCO MOSTO
p. 49, knee-length wool coat; p. 50, belted, robe, knee-length, double-breasted, princess, military; p. 52, fur

MP721/ZBP/ZUMA
p. 23, Claire Danes

NIKI NIKOLOVA/FILMMAGIC
p. 33, Sienna Miller, right

NPX/STAR MAX
p. 27, Demi Moore

LILLY PALMBERGER/ CELEBRITY PHOTO
p. 13, Eva Longoria, left; p. 27, Sharon Stone

DOUG PETERS/RETNA
p. 22, Jessica Simpson; p. 182, Diane Kruger

GEORGE PIMENTEL/WIREIMAGE
p. 59, Selma Blair

MARK PLATT
p. 115, dressy tank

QUEEN/RETNA
p. 16, Drew Barrymore, left

RETNA
p. 27, Cindy Crawford

ALISON ROSA
p. 80, hobo

DOUG ROSA
p. 154

LISA ROSE/JPI
p. 14, Salma Hayek, right; p. 22, Hilary Swank, Rosario Dawson; p. 25, Jessica Alba; p. 38, Angelina Jolie, right; p. 182, Gwen Stefani

JIM RUYMEN/UPI/LANDOV
p. 28, Oprah Winfrey

JOY E. SCHELLER/ LONDON FEATURES
p. 21, Naomi Watts

TOM SCHIERLITZ
p. 96, wristlet, chain, clutch, satin clutch; p. 97, vintage frame; p. 110, blazer, feminine; p. 111, sporty; p. 118; p. 119, scoopneck, long sleeve; p. 128; p. 129, all-day urban look; p. 134, shirred, print; p. 135, ruffled, two-tone; p. 138, flats; p. 164, cocktail ring, big cuff, p. 181, ring

ADRIAN SEAL/FILMMAGIC
p. 15, Kate Hudson, right

LISA SHIN
p. 69, shrug; p. 162 pendant necklace

STEPHEN SHUGERMAN/ GETTY p. 13, Eva Longoria, right

JIM SMEAL/BEIMAGES
p. 18, Queen Latifah, left

PAUL SMITH/FEATUREFLASH/ RETNA p. 182, Fergie

PAUL SMITH/RETNA
p. 27, Heather Locklear

AJ SOKALNER/ACE PICTURES/NEWSCOM
p. 36, Jennifer Lopez, right

JIM SPELLMAN/WIREIMAGE
p. 25, Jessica Biel

JOHN SPELLMAN/RETNA
p. 28, Anjelica Huston

SPLASH
p. 129, Charlize Theron

KARSTEN STAIGER
p. 49, to-the-knee-boots

BILL STEELE
p. 107, straw bag; p. 126, long shorts; p. 127, straw

DAN STEINBERG/BEIMAGES
p. 29, Goldie Hawn

STEINBERG/SVITOJUS/ABBOT/ INFGOFF
p. 73, Jennifer Aniston

ALBERTO TAMARGO/GETTY
p. 26, Eva Mendes

KARWAI TANG/ALPHA/GLOBE
p. 38, Angelina Jolie, left; p. 51, Renée Zellweger

MARK J. TERRILL/AP
p. 32, Sarah Jessica Parker, left

TIME INC. DIGITAL STUDIO
p. 49, A-line skirt, cardigan;
p. 54-57; p. 58, A-line skirt; p. 68,
cardigan, belted; p. 70-71; p. 74;
p. 75, back to work look on model;
p. 112-113; p. 124-125; p. 130;
p. 136, buckle; p. 139, embellished;
p. 160; p. 162, bangles; p. 165,
ethnic bracelets; p. 172, sundress,
beach bag, dressy thong; p. 183

UNO PRESS/WIREIMAGE.COM
p. 121, Keri Russell

**DENNIS VAN TINE/LONDON
FEATURES:** p. 16, Drew
Barrymore, right

JEFF VESPA
p. 32, Sarah Jessica Parker, right

JAMES WADE
p. 164, impact earrings

WENDELL T. WEBBER
p. 5; p. 43, shoes and shoe boxes,
shoe organizer, purses

CHRIS WEEKS/WIREIMAGE
p. 34, Joy Bryant, right

IAN WEST/PA/ ABACA
p. 17, Beyoncé Knowles, right

RAY WILLIAMS/CELEBRITY
p. 163, Ashley Judd

RICHARD YOUNG/REX
p. 75, Elle Macpherson

INDEX

A

Accents
  age and, 25, 28
  personal style and, 34
Age
  20s, 25
  30s, 26
  40s, 27
  50s, 28
  60s, 29
  dressing for your, 24–29
  jewelry and, 25
  playfulness and, 25
Alba, Jessica, *25*
Aniston, Jennifer, 35, *35, 72*

B

Bags
  attaché, 81, *81*
  beach tote, 137, *137*
  buckle, 136, *136*
  canvas, 136, *136*
  chain, 96, *96*
  clutch, 96, *96,* 136, *136*
  crescent, 81, *81*
  daytime, 80–81
  drawstring, 80, *80*
  evening, 96–97
  handheld, 80, *80*
  hobo, 80, *80*
  minaudiere, 97, *97*
  oblong, 80, *80*
  organizing, 43
  satin clutch, 96, *96*
  shopping for, 181
  straw, 137, *137*
  for travel, 169, 173
  trendproof, 177, *177*
  vintage, 185, *185*
  vintage frame, 97, *97*
  web sites for, 191
  work tote, 136, *136*

wristlet, 96, *96*
Bargaining, 184
Barrymore, Drew, 16, *16*
Beach wear, *172,* 172–173
Beckinsale, Kate, *23*
Bello, Maria, *22*
Belts, 43
Berry, Halle, 39, *39*
Beyoncé, 17, *17*
Beyond Basics, 153
  jewelry, 160–165
  lingerie and, 154–159
  travel, 166–175
Biel, Jessica, *25*
Bilson, Rachel, 37, *37*
Blair, Selma, *21, 59*
Blanchett, Cate, *26*
Body Type
  boyish
    dresses for, 19
    general principles for, 19
    ruffles for, 19
    shoes for, 19
    swimsuits for, 135, *135*
  busty
    dresses for, 16
    guiding principles for, 16
    shoes for, 16
    suits for, 16
  curvy
    blouses for, 17
    dresses for, 17
    guiding principles for, 17
    pants for, 17
  curvy/petite
    blouses for, 14
    colors for, 14
    dresses for, 14
    guiding principles for, 14
    jeans for, 14
  full-figured
    dresses for, 18
    guiding principles for, 18
    pants for, 18
    patterns for, 18
    swimsuits for, 134, *134*

pear shaped
    swimsuit for, 135, *135*
    tailoring for, 18
    v-neck for, 18
  petite
    blouses for, 14
    colors for, 14
    dresses for, 13, 14
    guiding principles for, 13, 14
    jeans for, 14
    shoes for, 13
  short legs, shoes for, 13
  slender/petite
    dresses for, 13
    guiding principles for, 13
    shoes for, 13
  small-busted
    dresses for, 15
    fabric for, 15
    guiding principles for, 15
    shirts for, 15
  thicker waist, swimsuits for,
    134, *134*
Bosworth, Kate, *25*
Boutiques
  in Atlanta, 186
  in Austin, 186
  in Boston, 186
  in Chicago, 186–187
  in Las Vegas, 187
  in Los Angeles, 187–188
  in Miami, 188–189
  in New York City, 189–190
  in Philadelphia, 190
  in San Francisco, 190
  in Seattle, 190
  vintage, 185
  in Washington, D.C., 190
Bras
  bust enhancer, 157, *157*
  bust minimizer, 156, *156*
  contour, 156, *156*
  convertible, 157, *157*
  fit of, 155
  low back, 157, *157*
  no underwire, 156, *156*

looks we love

ACKNOWLEDGMENTS

Kyle Acebo
Jonathan Ambar
Bozena Bannett
David Brown
Glenn Buonocore
Heidi Ernst
Sue Fan
Robert Marasco
Brooke McGuire
Jonathan Polsky
Holly Rothman
Nathan Sayers
Ilene Schreider
Lindsey Stanberry
Time Inc. Digital Studio
Shoshana Thaler
Adriana Tierno
Britney Williams
Megan Worman

JAIME KING IN DIOR